WOMEN IN REAL ESTATE WHO

WOMEN in Real Estate who Boss Up

Celebrating Boss Ladies who are making their mark in their industry and flourishing.

PRESENTED BY
Women With Vision International

First Printing, 2022

Book Interior Design by VMC Art & Design, LLC

ISBN: 979-8-9853309-3-9

Delucslife Media
Sheridan, WY

www.delucslife.com

Printed in USA

TABLE OF CONTENTS

FOREWORD

by Debbie Biery

"A woman's place is in the home."

THAT'S THE SUBTEXT THAT QUIETLY LINED THE halls of my school, the glossy pages of every magazine my friends and I flipped through, and the reflection I saw in the nightly sitcoms I watched with my sisters sitting together on our old brown couch.

But, ironically, my mom wasn't there.

Unlike my friend's moms, mine was out working multiple jobs in an attempt to make enough money to put food on the table.

When Caroline reached out to ask me to write the forward for this incredible collection of stories, I was honored. I scrolled through the manuscript with my mouth agape as I read her interview. What an incredible force of will, creativity, and work ethic Caroline possesses. No wonder she wanted to create a book to positively impact others.

While no one had a perfectly paved path to success, each woman in this book has navigated the bumps with grit and tenacity, followed their dream, and found their version of success.

These stories are what I wish a younger version of myself had access to as I was sitting on the couch with my sisters, figuring out my first business in college, or when I decided to embark on my real estate journey.

My choice to enter the world of real estate didn't come from a book but instead from a childhood friend. Her family was wealthy, they owned a lot of real estate, and I loved going to their houses (yes, plural). For me, it wasn't just about being in a beautiful space, it was about the feeling of safety and stability they seemed to have.

When I was 28 and had decided to adopt my son, I knew that I wanted that safety and stability for my growing family too. I thought back to the day my friend looked at me and said "Hey Debbie, I think you'd make a good realtor" and that was it. With the memory of those 7 words, there was no turning back.

My path had its bumps too, (my very first day at the office a successful, male agent came right up to me and said, "You will never make it as a real estate agent", I had relatives buy from other people instead of me, and I threw personal safety to the wind in the pursuit of making a sale). The list of bumps is extensive, however, I was not only able to find the safety and stability I had been looking for outside of me, but I was able to create it from within me.

Real estate allowed me to be in control of my earnings, to connect with people, and to sell something that was truly meaningful. To me, as corny as it may sound, every house sale was an opportunity for a home to be made, for people to be nourished, for gathering to happen.

It's what allowed me to create a life where I could sit on the couch with my son reading stories to help him dream while ensuring our house felt like home.

You see, stories are what connect us. Whether it's in your living room, over the island in the kitchen, or through the pages of a book. They give us hope, teach us lessons, and show us what's possible.

Throughout these pages, you'll find stories of real women who have done the inner and outer work required to become the person they are now.

Whether you're picking up this book as a seasoned real estate professional or with curiosity as you consider a real estate adventure, I want to share with you 3 things.

1. The location of where you work doesn't matter but the feeling of it does.

   When I became a realtor with eXp there were under 300 agents. Today, there are over 84,000. This growth didn't happen because of a catchy marketing strategy, it happened because of the true intention and connection this company fosters.

   Whether it's with eXp or somewhere else, I hope you find your professional home.

2. Sometimes a woman's place is **selling** the home.

   More accurately, her place is wherever the heck she wants it to be.

   For those women who want to make money, connect with and serve people, maintain the flexibility needed to be at home with the kids or traveling through Europe, or caring for your parents, or focusing on your mental health, I want you to know that pursuing a career in real estate is an exciting adventure full of challenges and rewards. Stay true to yourself while you follow your dreams.

3. And last but not least, remember that there is no such thing as perfection.

There will be challenges along the way, and those challenges are a sign that you are on the right path. Challenges are how we grow. You may fall down, you may experience "failure", but remind yourself that you are training your resiliency muscle and get back up.

May the stories in the following pages give you the hope you need, the belonging you long for, and the inspiration to keep going even if things feel hard.

For all the little girls who got the wrong message, it's time we show them, and ourselves what's possible and what it looks like to Boss Up.

Welcome home.

ABOUT DEBBIE BIERY

debbiebiery.com

Debbie Biery is a SUCCESS Brand Ambassador and Certified SUCCESS Coach with a 22 year career in real estate. She has played an active role in the expansion of eXp Realty including living in an RV while traveling the country promoting the company. She is a sought after speaker and serial entrepreneur passionate about encouraging women to get out of their own way.

She offers practical, how-to steps in her 'Dear

Debbie's column in SUCCESS Magazine and her vast experiences span from real estate to leadership development to business building and is woven together by the pursuit of making the world a better place for all. When she's not helping women unapologetically go after their dreams, you can find her playing with her family, boating, lifting weights, or painting. To learn more head to debbiebiery.com.

SECTION 1

Lifestyle

RIMA RAFEH
The Rafeh Group
Broker Associate/ Team Leader

CHAPTER 1

Surrounding Yourself with People that Can Change Your Life
with Rima Rafeh

HEY THERE, SUPERWOMEN. I AM SO EXCITED today to have my next guest. A lot of you know that my background is in real estate, and I have a special place in my heart for real estate. So I love speaking to a woman in the real estate industry. It's not common in certain parts of the real estate industry, but this amazing woman is recognized as a leading broker in Greater L.A. I know what that means, I've been in L.A. for over 22 years. She is distinguished among others with a wide array of experience in both residential and commercial real estate.

Q: Rima Rafeh, how are you?

Rima Rafeh: I am great. Thank you for having me. I'm excited.

Q: I am excited. Before I jump into this, I also want to mention that were just chatting about what an amazing athlete you are. Have you always been an athlete?

RR: Well, I've been working out for a very long time. I've always loved challenges and I wanted to challenge myself, challenge my body, and of course, challenge my mind. So a few years ago I start getting involved in these crazy things. I've done four marathons; I've done very, very long bike rides. I started with the Arthritis Foundation. They have an amazing ride from San Francisco to L.A. every year, and that's actually what got me into cycling. I'm like, "Why not? You do something exciting, fun, and challenging and you raise money for a great cause." So I've done that four or five times.

It's been amazing. Now I ride with a group of people, and I have a 500-mile ride coming up in two days. I'm not ready! I'm excited, but not ready, a little nervous. I did not train because I've been so busy with work. But yes, I love to challenge myself. I always like to look for something that's going to keep me on my toes and keep me moving.

Q: This is probably why you're so great in real estate, in the industry you've chosen. You like to constantly challenge yourself. You are consistently ranked in the top one percent of real estate professionals in the region and in 2021 you were voted Antelope Valley's Best Realtor. So this is who you are. You go for it. So let's look back a little bit. There are a lot of careers you could have chosen. Why real estate?

RR: Honestly, I did not wake up one day and say, "You

know what? I'm going to be a realtor." Sixteen, seventeen years ago, I used to do medical billing and insurance. It was an office job and honestly it was very boring. I was at my desk a lot. I found myself just dragging myself to work. I am very active. I like to move around a lot, talk to people on a fun level, not just, you know, hammering people for money and stuff like that.

So I always used to complain about my job and then a friend of mine and my sister-in-law were like, "Why don't you get into real estate?" I'm like, "Real estate?" I never pictured myself being a realtor or real estate agent. I didn't think I would be a good real estate agent. But they said, "Just go and get your license." And everybody was killing it back then, in 2006. That's when the conversation started. So I did it. I got my agent's license. Now I'm a broker, but I got my agent license first, passed the first time, and I jumped into it, not knowing what I was going to face.

Well, I started in 2007 and everybody knows what happened in 2007. When I was coming in, everybody was walking out the door, leaving the business. But I was determined to make it work and make it happen. Yes, I struggled, and it wasn't a fun couple of years as I was start-ing out. But it was the most rewarding experience and the most amazing field that I found I had a passion for, that I love doing. I wake up excited about the day and the clients and all the activities that go with it.

Q: That's amazing. Being a real estate broker in L.A., being a woman, this can't be an easy market. What are some of the ups and downs you have experienced, whether in life or in business?
RR: There are a lot of ups and a lot of downs with any

business. Being a woman, it's not always comfortable show-ing properties or going to an appointment. There's always that fear that comes with it. For me, the biggest challenge was just having these negative thoughts. Coming from a Middle Eastern background, as a Middle Eastern woman, you have what I call that drunk monkey in your brain. It's telling you that you're not going to make it, you're not worthy. It's not for us, as women, especially from the Middle East, to grow and nurture ourselves. I came with that mentality at the beginning. So it was a challenge to push myself and to believe in myself—to get to that point where I said, "I can make it. I can do it and I can show other women that it can happen. We can be successful no matter what our back-ground is, no matter what our history is." There is amazing opportunity, especially being in real estate, to make it work. And it was up to me to make it or break it.

So that was a big challenge, especially because I had family, too. I was married with children. My children were little at that time, so balancing life and business was a chal-lenge. I wanted to grow and flourish and succeed while also taking care of the family and being able to please everyone around me. And I don't know if you know any Middle Eastern people, but they like to party and socialize. And so it was a lot to deal with, honestly. I believe that was my biggest challenge to being here and having that success and being able to be what I am today.

Q: I want to take us a little bit further in this conversation because you did make it, you're doing it. We all see your success, but what did you have to do? What did you have do for yourself to get over the doubts?
RR: I had to learn to say no to a lot of things. Again, coming

from wanting to please everyone, I had to find that place where I was happy with myself and it was okay to say no. It was okay to say no to certain people. It was okay to say no to family, to my husband, to my children. And I know that I was doing it for everyone around me at the same time.

We think of it in reverse sometimes. We think what we're doing is hurting people. But what we are doing, actually, is helping people. You're able to contribute and give and have financial freedom. I mean, I read a lot. I work out a lot. I love nature. I love hiking. I cycle for a reason. I just forget the world and I have a lot of good thoughts (sometimes bad thoughts) in my head. It took a lot of self-discovery to get here, knowing that it is okay to be selfish a little bit.

That's what we struggle with as women. We feel like we're being selfish, but if we really discover what our self-ishness is all about, we will be able to proceed and move forward and make it happen.

Q: Amazing. What inspires you now?
RR: What inspires me has changed. Three years ago, I started a team. It had gotten to a point in real estate, where, yes, I was a top producer. I was killing it, closing deals. And three years ago I decided to start a team and now what inspires me the most is not the transactions and how many units we're going to close. Helping our clients and being there for them definitely is a big plus, but it's amazing to now have a lot of agents around me and helping them grow.

Helping them to provide for their families, for their loved ones and watching their journey is inspiring. Most of my agents are brand new agents; they started with me fresh. And having that person start from zero and then build them to be top producers, it's the most phenomenal feeling. That's what really drives me every day. I get up to be here for my team, be here for our clients, and just make things happen and change lives. We change lives for the better.

Q: One of the things that I love about you is, of course, everyone wants to be a part of a winning team. They want to be associated with a winner. So I'm sure just being around you is inspiring and motivating to your agents. What would you tell a new agent, especially a woman, who is just starting in this industry? She doesn't know if she's going to make it or not. What would you tell her to do to be successful, to get in there and start making it happen as you did?

RR: I would definitely say get with another successful woman. For the longest time, I was so intimidated by people who were successful because I felt so small. Like if I got in a room with top agents, I would think, "Oh, my God, I'm going to say something stupid" or "They are going to think that I'm stupid, I don't have any transactions under my belt." I thought they would look up my numbers, I had all these negative thoughts in my mind.

And now things have changed in my life, too. Now I want to be the smallest fish in the room. I want to be the idiot. I want to be the one who doesn't know much. I want to surround myself with giants. And I advise every single woman not to be intimidated. We're all here to help each other. Surround yourself with the people—with that woman who is going to take you to a higher level. That woman who is going to be there for you, who is like, "Hey, I did this wrong. You better do this and this and this."

Take everything in, don't take anything personally.

Again, I learned from my mistakes, I used to take things personally. I thought people were judging me or they were saying things to hurt me. But I mean, get over it. We are here for each other. The right person can change your life. We've all been through things, every woman goes through a struggle, whether in life or in business. So just definitely surround yourself with the right people, the right woman.

Q: I agree. I know someone is listening to this and they have been thinking about real estate, thinking about doing something new. You're with an amazing real estate group, that's really all over the world. But if someone's in a different market, can they still join your team?

RR: Yes, of course. I am with eXp Realty. We have a team that serves most of L.A. Wherever you are, whether you want to join my team or not, we're here to help each other. We're always on Zoom with training and coaching. Do you want a one-on-one with me? I am an open book. So whether you are involved in my team, you'd like to join my team, or you just want to have a conversation, I would love nothing more than to help anybody out there.

Q: I love it. Where can they find you? Would they reach out to you on your website?

RR: Yes, the website is rimarafeh.com. And they can find me on my personal Instagram @rimarafeh1. My business is @TheRafehGroup. And my Facebook and YouTube channel are under my name, Rima Rafeh.

Q: Thank you so much, Rima. This has been amazing.

RR: Thank you for having me. Love it.

RIMA RAFEH
www.rimarafeh.com

Rima Rafeh is recognized as a leading Real Estate Broker in the Greater Los Angeles area, distinguished among others with a wide array of experience in both residential and commercial real estate. As an active REALTOR® since 2007 and team leader of The Rafeh Group brokered by eXp Realty, Rima prides herself on her extensive market expertise and unmatched devotion to clients.

Rima is consistently ranked among the top 1% of real estate professionals in the region also voted AV's best Realtor for 2021 with expertise directly translating to more than $250,000,000 in sales within the local market. The Rafeh Group brokered by eXp Realty shares their passion for perfection and adoption of innovation to deliver both real-world results and an enjoyable experience.

As an avid runner and cyclist, Rima continuously supports worthy causes and nonprofit organizations. Most notably, her philanthropic efforts have included running multiple marathons and participating in a 550-mile bicycle ride from San Francisco to Los Angeles.

Beyond leading an active lifestyle and a renowned team of professionals, her greatest accomplishment is being a devoted mother of 3 and living life to the fullest with purpose.

I advise every single woman not to be intimidated. We're all here to help each other. Surround yourself with the people who are going to take you to a higher level.

—Rima Rafeh

REBECCA SOTO

Soto Legacy Group, Realtor

CHAPTER 2

Do More of What Sets Your Heart on Fire

with Rebecca Soto

HEY THERE, SUPERWOMEN. I AM SO EXCITED today to have my next guest. I just met her and we have been having some of the greatest conversations. She's a little unique. My parents were business owners, they worked together, and that was one of the things I looked up to my whole life. They owned their own business. They had real estate, they did home improvement, and I always wanted that in my life. And now that's what I have. I work with my husband. So when I meet another woman who is part of another couple who had that same vision, who has that same experience, it's just a joy. It lets you know it's possible. So I'm excited to talk about how she created her business and how she likes working with her spouse.

Q: Rebecca Soto, how are you?
Rebecca Soto: Hi, I'm doing good. Thank you so much for having me.

Q: Yes. I'm excited to have this conversation because a lot of people think, "Oh, I couldn't work with my husband. How can you do that?" But I think it's so much fun to work with him. Maybe it's our personalities. But let's start with how you got into the real estate industry in the first place.

RS: It's interesting because in my early twenties, I was a receptionist for a real estate broker. But fast forward, I ended up working as a dental assistant and I did that for many years. It's how I met my husband, which I talk about in my book, *Married In Real Estate*, but I met him through that. Shortly after, we got married—he was a truck driver at the time, and I remember thinking, "I just want to do something that's more meaningful." And having just bought a house, like many other people, I realized this could be something that we could both work on together. And I knew I would love to be able to help other families find their dream homes, or even work with people who were looking for investment property or vacation homes.

I mean, we live in the vacation capital here in Orlando, Florida. So we thought, "You know what? We should give this a try." And so both of us embarked on this and got our licenses at the same time. We didn't go cold turkey, you know, leaving our day jobs. Because I don't know if you're aware, there's a transitional period there, where we had to put in a lot of extra hours working two jobs to be able to build that business. But it's been amazing so far.

Q: How many years have you been working in real estate now?
RS: It's been 16 years. Since 2006.

Q: What ingredient do you think it takes? Because I've often thought about this. What ingredient do you think it takes to work with your spouse?
RS: Well, we wanted to be able to spend more time together, so I think our desires were aligning, right? We wanted to be available to our young family and be able to work around that schedule. Both of us having 9-to-5s, it was hard to be there for the kids, for their field trips and karate or basketball, gymnastics, whatever they were in, it was challenging. So we saw an opportunity where we could do this together, try it out and see if it worked. The ingredient would be aligning our vision.

Q: That's really, really cool. What were some of the ups and downs that you faced? Whether in life or in creating that business?
RS: The truth is, we work really well together. Challenges would be that the market is ever changing. We came in right before the market crash, and those were just hard times for everybody, no matter where you were, a lot of people were losing their jobs. There were a lot of people who were losing their homes. And so even though we are both driven and we are doing whatever we can to make that living, it does get challenging at times. It challenges your

marriage, it challenges your family, it challenges your ability to keep up with your finances. We really did go through a lot of hardship financially, which was all pulling at us, but the truth is, our hearts were still always aligned.

You can get into the blame game of who's working more, who's working less, but knowing that you're one team and you're on the same side, I think, is what helped us get through all of it, you know? Having been through that crash and seeing the market shifts now, I feel like it has certainly made it a lot easier because there's nothing to surprise you. You know that if you are willing to roll with the punches and make changes in your life, you're going to be okay. And I think that goes for any industry. You have to be willing to make changes when things aren't the same, right?

Q: Yes. What inspired you to write a book about it?
RS: I'll tell you, it wasn't on my radar initially, but I met someone who came to be a speaker at one of our events. He spent the day with us and just seeing the dynamics of how we work together, he was so intrigued by our relationship, how we coordinated, how well we worked together, that he was like, "You guys honestly need to write a book." And I sat and I thought about that. We'd been married, at that moment, 20 years. We were celebrating our 20th anniversary, and I thought, yes, that would be a good idea to share with people all the things that we've been through, our ups and downs. And I hoped that it would be of some value to help get someone through hard times and see how we got through some of those challenges that we went through in our life.

Q: So good. My husband and I wrote a book together as well, it's called *The Right End of the Chase*. We wrote it about our dating experience, and we are thinking we should write the second in that series. *The Right End of the Chase in Marriage*. And so I love these kinds of stories and seeing couples be able to create their life this way. What is inspiring you right now?

RS: After we wrote this book—and the truth is, there was no market research to know if anyone was even interested in the topic—but I'll tell you, once it was out there, it was so well received. And of course, now we also have a podcast, "Married in Real Estate," and the responses on there were overwhelming as well, because it is a topic that a lot of people appreciate. I think it's bringing those values back into that working married relationship. It's a subject that is not widely spoken about. Not that it's a taboo, it's kind of overlooked, right? And the truth is, most people in our industry realize they're at a disadvantage sometimes when their spouse is not in the industry, because they don't understand the nature of the business. It might be frustrating to get calls at all hours of the day, or you're going to show a property on the weekend and you're hoping your significant other would have a 9-to-5 so that they could shut it off.

And so there is an advantage when your spouse is working with you in the industry because they just understand. You don't have to deal with the explanation or the setbacks that you can sometimes face. But that can be a gift and a curse. So I think the support group is really important because while we're all so understanding, sometimes that can go overboard and then you're working overtime and you don't know when to shut it off. And so there's a lack of balance sometimes, and no one else understands that.

Q: Yes.

RS: I think that's what keeps me going, is knowing that the message that we are putting out there—and all we do is have meaningful conversations with other working couples who share what's working for them, what's not working, challenges that they've had and how they've overcome them. And I feel like that has had a really great response or it resonates well with the audience that's watching.

Q: You know, Rebecca, since I've been growing my boss-up community, I've noticed that a lot of high-achieving women, not all of them, but a lot of them, have their spouses in their business. I've been noticing this trend happening where the woman might be the CEO, she might have been the brains of the whole operation, but then her husband is the operations person or the marketing person or something like that. It's been interesting to see it happening. I'm here because I love working with my husband. What would you tell another woman, married or not, what is your advice for becoming successful or growing a business?

RS: I think you really need to just search your heart. Discover what sets your heart on fire and just try to do more of whatever that is. If it's real estate, then there's a lot of things and people who will scare you out of it—and there'll be people who scare you into it! So I would say surround yourself with people who support your ideas, or people who are already in that industry that are going to be a great guide for you and help lift you up. Because if you don't surround yourself with people who are positive, uplifting, or already in that industry, there's so many conflicting opinions and people who just scare you. And so I think that would be the one important thing. Really surround yourself with people who are going to help elevate you.

Q: I love that. Do you find yourself attracting more people who are the same as you, couples who are working together, or is it all over the board?

RS: I would say all over the board, because even though, yes, we do attract some other working couples, I think overall there's an appreciation for the values, whether you're married or not. And then also knowing that there's someone that you can reach out to when you do have certain questions, right? I think that's something that—again, it's not a taboo, but it's not widely spoken about, so you don't really know who you can talk to. And so knowing that person is there, it's a relief to have somebody that can hear you out or somebody who can give you some guidance. After I started doing my own research, I found a lot of amazing books on the topic, but I wasn't even aware of it before. So it's in my research that I've come across a lot of amazing books. And now you told me about yours, so I'm excited to look that one up. Definitely looking forward to that.

Q: What advice would you give couples or teams working together?

RS: This advice is good for anyone working with someone else.

Get clear on your vision—each person should write down what they want to accomplish or achieve in the next 12 months. Then bring those visions together in one vision board. Create ONE Vision, ONE Plan of Action.

Surround yourself with positive people who are where you want to be and support your vision and goals. Remove or limit negative people.

Design your Roles! Play to your strengths and focus on the one thing that lights you up! Hire others to do the things you are not good at or that are not dollar productive for you to do. Your time is valuable!

Create a schedule and stick to it! Start at a consistent time each day and end at a consistent time!If you do not run the day, the day will run you! You deserve personal time and time with your Family! Most of us work to provide a wonderful life for our family, but the best thing you can give them is your undivided quality time.

Find a community! Feel free to join our Facebook Group, Married In Real Estate.

Q: **Another thing just came to me, which is a benefit to knowing someone like you or just connecting with someone like you. Let's say you're in real estate and you don't have your spouse in it with you. Having you there, you understand some of the things that happen with your spouse. And your husband is there. Sometimes when you have events and you have that person come and bring their husband, now the husband understands the lifestyle a little bit more because he's there. This happens a lot with me. My husband is always at my events, and a lot of women bring their husbands. And all of a sudden, it just becomes much more clear about what you do and they don't get as threatened by it, or something gets shifted by having you both there.**

So hats off to you for doing this. It would be beneficial for anyone to reach out to you, whether they have questions about having their spouse work with them or just to talk to you, knowing that you're married and you have the values that you have, how you've become successful and how you manage your life. How can people find out more about you, your team, your book?

RS: I've got two websites. The first one is SotoLegacyGroup.

work, and that's my digital business card. You can see all of our YouTube channels there, there's a Calendly so that we can connect and do a coaching call, or you can link to my websites. But if you're interested in the book, then it's MarriedinRealEstate.com.

Q: I love it, Rebecca. Thank you so much. I look forward to all the stuff we're going to be doing together.
RS: Thank you. I look forward to it as well.

REBECCA SOTO
www.MarriedInRealEstate.com

Rebecca Soto leads a real estate team alongside her husband. Together they have grown their real estate organization working together since 2006, serving the Central Florida area.

She has focused on serving the real estate community through leadership, education, and mentoring.

Earned awards such as eXp's Icon Agent, Orlando Real Producers Top 500 agents, 2019 Top Orlando Couples, and NAHREP's Top 250 Latino Real Estate Agents

Leading their local agents they have now expanded their organization into Several states and 6 countries and several states nationwide!

During the pandemic, Rebecca and her husband took some time to write a book, Married In Real Estate where they journal their life experience working together in real estate as a married couple. It's told with Her Side and His Side of Love, Financial Ruin, Success & Working Together To Create their Ever After. Now with this opportunity, she gets to dive deep and share as a woman how she rose to success in real estate as a wife, mother, grandmother helping others also find success in the industry.

So much can be learned from reading their story, the book comes with Life Lessons and exercises to reflect on your journey. For a limited time, they are offering the book for FREE at www.MarriedInRealEstate.com

You really need to just search your heart. What sets your heart on fire just try to do more of whatever that is.

—Rebecca Soto

NICOLE MAJORS
BeMAJOR Team, Team Leader

CHAPTER 3

Mindset is The Name of the Game to Make You Limitless

with Nicole Majors

HEY THERE, SUPERWOMEN. I AM SO EXCITED today to have my next guest. As you know, I'm excited to be launching a whole new series in real estate because I was in real estate for 21 years. I have referenced this on the podcasts many times! I'm peculiar in that I find real estate sexy. I was in it for a long time, in marketing and in operations, and so this series is exciting to me because when I was in real estate, I didn't always see women on the commercial side. So to see these powerful women who are doing such amazing things in the industry is inspiring. My guest today is from Port St. Joe, Florida, she's been in real estate a while, and we're going to hear about how her company works and why she loves this industry.

Q: Nicole Majors, welcome.
Nicole Majors: Thank you. I am excited.

Q: I'm so excited to have you. There are a lot of ways people come into real estate. I don't know if it's one of those things that people grow up thinking about doing—
NM: I don't think so.

Q: No. People fall into it. So how did you find yourself closing deals in real estate? What brought you to the industry?
NM: I'm originally from Kansas. A really, really small town in Kansas. I grew up on a farm. When I met my husband, his mom was working at the county courthouse and she hooked me up with a job at a local title company. I started off filing, literally just doing some filing back in those days before everything was electronic. But I'm a person that will continually find ways to grow and evolve and do something bigger and better. So I spent about eight years with this title company and by the end, I was a closing agent and I was the one that took the lenders and the buyers and the sellers and everyone into one room and made them very happy. And either everyone walked out with a check or with keys. I mean, something amazing was happening, right?

After that, we raised our children and we ended up taking custody of our nephew and raising our nephew. So I went back to working a little closer to home. I worked in banking, insurance and even started a business from scratch. Then, when we got the opportunity to move to Florida, my husband said, "You've done a lot of things, what is the one thing that you really enjoyed?" And I said, "I loved working for the title company." But there wasn't anyone here hiring for that. So I got started with a local real estate company here, working first as an assistant, but immediately I got my real estate license, and worked up to an Inside Sales Agent (ISA) role, then moved up to a buyer's agent.

Again, I'm a person who wants to continue to grow and learn and succeed and help others succeed. So since then I've started my own team and now I have four people under me. I'm assisting others to raise them up into real estate and I love every second of it. It's fantastic. It's a good time.

Q: Real estate is a good time. You're affecting the biggest decision in someone's life. The decisions that people make around real estate are always connected to something important, like their children's future.
NM: Yes. Most definitely.

Q: What do you like the most about growing a team and working with people? There's so much. What is your favorite part?
NM: There are a couple of favorite parts. I recently closed a $2.25 million sale and that was fantastic. And just to see them find that—and it's their second home, it's not their primary. I love that second home market, that investment market, that luxury market, it's really fun. And those clients are a little bit more analytical, typically. We're looking at numbers and we're diving deep into spreadsheets and things. And I kind of dig that. I'm a little bit nerdy that way.

But, I also recently closed with a wonderful gal named Cherie. They've been renting for years and we found a way for her to now be a homeowner for the very first time. Her kids are living in their home and it's cheaper than paying rent. And so there are those beautiful parts of explaining how great it is to become a homeowner and really taking it way back to those fundamentals and teaching people. Such as, this is what a survey is and this is what it does; this is what a home inspection is. Really helping those buyers who are very green, who are scared—I love that, too, it warms my heart.

And then, of course, now as a team leader I'm getting to see my agents rise up and do the same. And that light you get to see when your clients walk into a home and you just know it is the right one. This is the same light that I get to see with my team when they understand something or they get something closed. And I feel that same happiness, oh, my heart just grows 10 times bigger. You know, I'm so excited for them. I saw a post the other day from my coach which really hit home, it said "You can't compete with me because I'm cheering for you." I want you to win. So it's just so good. And it's such a good place for me to be mentally. I'm enjoying every second.

Q: I love that. What are some ups and downs you have experienced in your life and your business? Because as it relates to me in real estate, they were connected. Some of my ups in life were connected to real estate. Some of my downs in life were connected to real estate. What about you?
NM: Well, this is where you're going to understand why we have the name that we have. My team is the BeMAJOR team. And as far as the ups and downs on the business side, there's always that cyclical element. Coming from something that was very stable to now I'm team-leading—and it's very stable. I'm doing very well, but now I have these four people who are

dependent upon me and that can sometimes be a little heavy. But I do a lot of mindset work. I do yoga six times a week so that I can keep my sanity. So there are ways to do that.

On a personal level, I grew up in a very small town. And with very, I'll say, small thinkers. Most grow up there, marry someone from there, work, raise a family and eventually retire there. Which is fine, but I always wanted something more… something different. I promised my husband we would raise our daughters in one location. That time came, we made our move to Florida and Real Estate is where I landed. Our daughters are now 26 and 23. I've raised my kids, so as a parent with older children, I feel like it's a little easier for me to dive deep into real estate to give a little bit more every day, I can really get into the grind because I don't have small children to deal with. We also helped raise our nephew. We took custody of him when he was 11. Then between his sophomore and junior year he transitioned back to living with his mom, but he was still living in the same town that we were. It was quite an experience to raise a young man.

And so I hold a little stock in that kid. His name is Brandon and he was a big brother to our girls. We lost him to suicide in 2015. And that was the hardest thing as a family that we have ever been through. Before his death, Brandon had started this little company selling beard oils and other things. And he had this little saying, "Be Major," because he was Brandon Majors. So be major, be more, do more for others. He was a giver. He had such a spirit of love. And so from that point on our family kind of took that and we became the little "BeMAJOR" team.

Q: Yes. I love that.
NM: We've been using this "slogan" for years and I felt like

this last year I was strong enough to share this story and share the momentum behind it. And so when I created my team, I had to come up with a team name and I had one agent with me and I was telling him, like, I have to figure it out. And we were just talking about this, that, and the other. And I said the loss of Brandon was our catapult to do something different because life is just too dang short. It's just too short to sit here and not experience more than what we are in right now. So it just came to be. One night I woke up in the middle of the night thinking, "We're going to be the BeMAJOR team."

And so I sat down and wrote the values and principles and standards behind this. And that is where our team is and that's what we do. So my darkest moments as a family have become our brightest space right now. So I'm really excited to take what we have learned as a family and bring it forward to others.

Q: Thank you so much for sharing that. I feel like I want to take that on. I think we all should take that on actually. Be Major, don't be minor. There's another saying, "Don't major in minor things."

NM: There are a couple of things that we do. Our hashtags are: be inspiring, be amazing, be different, be kind, be loving, be fun. And we always want to Be Major, and what that means for us is we're going to be more for ourselves, each other and our clients. Whatever that looks like on a personal level or business level, we will hold ourselves to doing more for our community and doing more for others.

One of my team members said he was having a bad day recently and I said, "Are you having a bad day or did you just have a bad 10 minutes?" Because you can take what happened and let it define your day or you can let it go, and we're moving on because let's focus on what has happened that's been really good for you? And he's like, "OK."

Q: It's just good.
NM: You didn't have a bad day, you had a bad moment.

Q: Yes. This is so rich.
NM: Welcome to the thoughts in my head.

Q: Just think about that. Some jewels are being dropped here, oh, my goodness. What keeps you inspired?
NM: Honestly, my girls. I think, as moms, if you're a working mom, you have that real mom guilt about, "Gosh, I'm missing so much because I'm working," you know? I felt that, but what I'm feeling with adult children is that my girls, who are now adults and in the workforce, have so much respect. And they feel very inspired by watching their mom just go to the grind. And so every day what I do is because I know I have them watching me, and others, my team, everyone.

And the pressure, you know, creates the diamond. So I'm okay with a little bit of pressure. You can put some pressure on me. I'm okay. I've got this. I'm just going to keep moving forward. But I also look forward to the future and one day I'm going to have grandchildren and I want to make sure that what I leave is a legacy for my children and my grandchildren.

There's that song that talks about blessings upon you, your children, your children's children, and their children. That's what I want. I want to just inspire as best as I can and then let it grow out from there. If I can just inspire one of them, you know, to carry on to the next generation.

Q: Yes. Say that saying one more time.

NM: It's a song—sorry, I play the bass guitar and I sing, so I'm really into music! It's another one of my side gigs. The song is "The Blessing" by Cody Carnes, Elevation Worship and Kari Jobe. It is basically a blessing and the lyrics say, "May His favor be upon you and a thousand generations, and your family and your children and their children, and their children. I feel it's so important to bestow blessings on others and let it carry on. If you can teach something to just this one generation here, then they have the opportunity to pass it along.

Q: It'll ripple out. That's so good. What would you tell a woman who wants to really boss up in her business? Or what do you tell your team they need to focus on to be successful?

NM: For me personally, it is the mindset. I hired a coach. Initially, I thought I was hiring her for nutrition and physical training and, I said, "Let's get strong!" And that was part of it. But she really became more of a life coach. Her name is Angelica Ventrice and she's still out there coaching. Her business is called "Fit for Life" and it is designed specifically for busy businesswomen. And she works with a lot of real estate agents. But she works first and foremost on your mindset. Because if your mind isn't in play, the rest of it's not going to come into it. Initially, I had thought, "Oh, I got this, I've heard Tony Robbins a couple of times."

Q: Right.

But you have to be consistent. I read Brene Brown's book *Dare to Lead* and her *Braving the Wilderness*. I love all of that stuff. Her newest book is very, very deep.

So you have to eat healthy but you also need to think healthy. You need to have healthy things coming into your mind. Mindset is the name of the game. If you can get your mind wrapped around it, then you're limitless. I still have lots of work to do, but I've come so far in the last seven years and I'm just grateful for everyone who's taken just a small moment to be in my life, or as I call it my "bus ride of life."

Q: Is there anything else that you would share, that you have picked up along the way in your life that you would share with our audience? What have you really used to reach your level of success?

NM: I quit listening to the story that others were telling me about how I should live. I don't ever regret growing up on a farm in a small town. I don't regret getting up at 5 a.m. and going to help grandpa feed the cattle or in the middle of winter, digging into the pond to break the ice. I don't regret a moment of that small-town life.

But we can limit ourselves by the story that other people tell us and the story we tell ourselves. And the moment that we decided to rewrite this story was a moment where doors just really opened up. And when I say doors, it was barn doors opening up for us. It was insane. I took a step of faith and I was just, like, "Lord, if this is where we're supposed to go, and this is what I'm supposed to be doing, I'm on my way. Let's go." So I just went for it. I feel like so many times we hold ourselves back because we think, "I don't know if I can do that." And there are days when I wake up and I'm like, "What's going on?"

But I'm so excited. And as I say, feeling a little bit of pressure in your shoulders will really refine you into the person that you're supposed to be. But get people behind you. Make sure your circle is cheering for you. You have to have those people who are right there next to you, whatever comes, because things are going to get rough, but it's going to be good.

Q: I love that.
NM: But I would just go for it. Don't hesitate.

Q: Don't hesitate. Nicole, how can people find you? I know you are with eXp Realty. But tell us your website, tell us how they can connect with you on social media.
NM: Sure. So I'm in a little town called Port St. Joe, Florida. I moved from one small town to the next. But this small town is a little bit bigger—we have two stop lights in the town, so whoop, go us! We're called the "forgotten coast." A lot of people will have heard of Mexico Beach. Mexico Beach suffered Hurricane Michael in 2018. It kind of put us on the map, not a real good reason, but it is recovering beautifully, by the way. So I have an agent on my team who handles Panama City, Panama City Beach, and then we also cover Gulf and Franklin Counties as well, Port St. Joe, Cape San Blas. This whole area here. So we're a big investment/second-home market, but we do have a primary home space here. So on Facebook, I'm Nicole Majors and then we have the BeMajor Team. On Instagram, it is @bemajorteam_exprealty and the website is nicolemajors.exprealty.com. And I'm also one of those rare agents who really answers her phone: (850) 247-8415. Just call me or text me. I'm happy to get on the phone. I'll chat.

Q: Perfect. And if you're looking to get into real estate or if you're looking to invest, definitely connect, especially if you're interested in her market. Nicole, thank you. I look forward to everything we're doing.
NM: I'm so excited about what we're doing and I'm very honored to be a part of it.

NICOLE MAJORS
www.nicolemajors.exprealty.com

Nicole Majors has been in the real estate since 2015. Aside from years as a closing agent for a local title company in Kansas, Nicole has enjoyed a few brief careers in insurance and banking.

After a year of life changes, Nicole and her family moved to Port St Joe, Florida and found her love of real estate and has continued to grow and learn her craft. She re-branded herself and created a team in December of 2021 and grew the team to serve the local community.

The BeMAJOR team has a mission to be more than just a realtor for the clients they have the privilege to work with. The team strives to be caring, loving, inspiring and educational for all those they meet.

Nicole sold over $20 million as a buyer's agent only in a previous brokerage and has broke that ceiling in 2022 by June. She has also been named an eXp ICON in a short 6 months with the exp Realty brokerage and was able to cap in less than two months her first year with eXp.

Her passion is to partner with agents who are humble, hungry and willing to learn. Nicole enjoys watching others succeed in the business that has created a life for her family to enjoy.

Nicole and her husband, KC have raised two amazing daughters, Kaleigh and Kyla and are now enjoying the "empty nest". The BeMAJOR team is named in honor of their nephew Brandon, who passed January of 2015. The passion, love and desire to see others succeed is in his memory.

Get those people behind you, and make sure your circle is cheering for you. Whatever comes, just go for it, don't hesitate.

—Nicole Majors

It all comes down to your mindset, your hustle, and your priorities. If you have a drive, then anyone can be successful.

—*Kim Dean*

KIM DEAN
Simply Texas Real Estate Group
Founder, CEO and Associate Broker

CHAPTER 4

Having the Drive, Mindset, Hustle and priorities Makes you Successful

with Kim Dean

HEY THERE, SUPERWOMEN. I AM SO VERY EXCITED today to have my next guest. She is an amazing realtor from Texas and the owner of Simply Texas Real Estate Group. As I've mentioned many times, I have a history with real estate but she and I have even more in common because she also has a background in pharmaceuticals. It's funny because I initially wanted to be in pharmaceutical sales.

Q: Kim Dean, how are you?
Kim Dean: I'm great. Thanks so much for having me.

Q: I'm excited to have you here. When I looked at your bio, I thought, wow, we have crossed some paths that are similar. So you had a brief stint as a pharmaceutical sales rep.
KD: Yes.

Q: But you graduated with a degree in Agribusiness and Speech Communication.
KD: Yes.

Q: So let's hear about how that led you to the path of pharmaceutical sales and then real estate. What had you originally imagined your career path would be?
KD: I went to college thinking I was going to have one career path, but then I graduated with an entirely different one. What I ended up doing 5, 10, and then 15 years down the road was completely different from that! I went to Texas A&M University—I'm an Aggie and I love Texas A&M, love that school—and I went there because I thought I was going to be a veterinarian. I quickly realized that all of those science and math classes were just not my jam. I was having too much fun on the social scene. So I pivoted. I shifted and graduated with a degree in Agribusiness and Speech Communication. What's funny, though, is my first job out of college was in pharmaceutical sales for an animal health division of Novartis, which is a pharmaceutical company. I was now selling to veterinarians - ironic. I found myself on the other side, so it was a bit of a weird twist of fate on that.

Q: That's interesting. I want to stop right here and talk about how a lot of times people go to college and have a specific career path in mind. I was the same way. I started off going to school for chemistry. I don't even like chemistry and I'm not very great at science, so that wasn't going to work. And then I thought, okay, let me just do pharmacy. And I had this whole idea around pharmacy and that didn't work. So I ended up doing marketing. And at the time I thought, well, maybe I could do pharmaceutical sales, and that would be close enough. But no, I didn't end up doing that either. I took some detours along the way before I got to where I was supposed to be. So you graduated and you started working in pharmaceutical sales. Then what happened?

KD: My sales territory was in Dallas, which was perfect. From the age of three, I'd lived in North Texas, so I consider myself Texan. I graduated, moved back to Dallas to begin my career in pharmaceutical sales - and then my world flipped upside down when my mom ended up passing away three months to the day after I graduated from college. She has been a huge influence in my life. However almost every memory I have of her involves her being sick and chronically ill. But during the last four years of her life following her double lung transplant she was the healthiest I'd ever seen her. So she got to see me graduate from college. She got to see my baby brother graduate from high school. She even got to meet her first grandchild.

Her passing definitely impacted my path moving forward. Because of that, I became a lot more bold and adventurous in the decisions that I was going to make. One week before she passed I met my ex-husband. He was in the military and we had a very quick relationship. We ended up getting married and I very unexpectedly found out that I was expecting. I hadn't even been at my pharmaceutical sales job a year when I found myself married, pregnant and moving to the D.C. area where he was stationed. When I was nine months pregnant 9/11 happened. We were living one mile from the Pentagon, so I found myself once again facing tragedy but this time it was living out 9/11 through the eyes of living in the heart of the D.C. Metro area. After I gave birth to my son I had to take a brief hiatus. I thought to myself, I'm just going to be at home with my son. I had been through so much and wasn't expecting any of this. It was too soon for everything - to have children, get married - I wasn't ready—or so I thought. Are we ever really ready, though, to have kids?

Q: No, we're not.
KD: From that moment I said we're going to roll with this. And I just knew two things. One, I knew that I wanted to be a very active part of my children's lives, and two, I knew even in the first few weeks after my son was born that I was not one of the moms who was content to just be at home. I had to have a creative outlet. And that's really what brought me to real estate. There was a Century 21 flyer posted in our building on base and it said come tonight and learn all the ins and outs of being in real estate. I went and that was that. I haven't looked back since.

Q: Wow. You know, I've talked to so many different women and most of their major decisions are a result of children. You think about what house you need to get, what job you should take, the time off you need. It's all really based on the children. It sounds like you're the exact same. And it sounds like this ended up being the perfect thing for you as well.
KD: It was, and who knew? I mean, in that one year, from

the time I graduated and my mom passed away—I had lived through so much. I've heard that there's a list of the 10 most stressful things that you go through in your life, and when I looked back at that year I had knocked out seven of them! But those things put me on the path that I'm on now. And I don't know that I would've made a lot of the same decisions had those things not happened. Being a mom definitely changes your perspective and priorities in life and I am so blessed that it happened the way that it did.

Q: Yes. That's so good. I know it had to be tough, starting a business and doing it around kids. I mean, that's never easy.
KD: Right.

Q: What are some of the ups and downs that you had to experience? I lost my mom in 2016 and that changes everything for a lot of us. But what are some of the difficult things you had to get through just building your business and your life?
KD: I jumped into real estate by joining a team. I knew that I wanted to be in it, but I'm not one of the people who can do half-assed things, if I can say that. And so I started by joining a team because I wanted to learn from people who had already been successful in the business. I did this part-time while my son was in preschool. So the balancing act begins, right? Being able to balance work and home life is a struggle, and I think a lot of women are made to feel that they have to choose one or the other. That they either have to be at home or they have to go 60 hours a week.

I really felt from a very early age that you could do both. I'm very passionate to this day about helping women begin in real estate way earlier than they think they should so that they can lay the groundwork to have a thriving business later on. For me, I started my career on a team with a major franchise and it was perfect for that stage of my career. I got to learn a lot in a very hands-on fashion, seeing the ways I wanted to work my business and the ways I didn't. During my time on the team, our team lead opened up a RE/MAX franchise so I even got to witness behind the scenes what was involved in opening your own brokerage.

Right about this time I had my second son. It was 2007 and by then my sister had joined our real estate team. I loved this! I was working with my family. Towards the end of the year we were looking at our business plan. It was a crazy time in the real estate market. If you've read or seen "The Big Short" you know what I mean. We were evaluating where our business came from, our expenses, our profit and we noticed that a lot of our business was coming from things that we were doing to generate our own leads. Not necessarily from the brokerage, not necessarily from team leads, but from ourselves. Two moms. Two sisters - doing real estate how we wanted to.

And so it was about the time that the economy imploded in 2008 that she looked at me and said, "Go get your broker's license. Let's do our own thing." I prayed about it, we looked at the numbers, and we figured out that even if we did half the amount of business, we were going to make the same amount of money because we wouldn't have the splits with team members and the brokerage. That was the catalyst for becoming an entrepreneur. I fell in love with entrepreneurship even more at that point. We started our own independent boutique brokerage. What we thought at that point was just for the two of us. We thought, "Hey, maybe someday our kids might want to do this. Maybe they'll take it over." We never had the intention to grow that business; however, what we found was the agents we were working with on the other side of the transactions loved working with us. They started to reach out and ask, hey, are you guys hiring? So my sister and I took one look at each other, and said, okay! Why not?

We had to figure out so many things. What were our splits going to be? What is our compensation plan? What are we providing? But we just kind of rolled with it and figured it out. We always asked ourselves, "how do we want to be treated?"...and made decisions through that lense. It was one of the best decisions we ever made. I don't think a lot of people have the guts to do that. It's scary, but we knew it was right for us. Our priorities were family first, business second. We knew that we were laying the groundwork for our future when the kids weren't little anymore. We knew eventually the day would come when they're going to grow up and move on. Business will always be there...but school dances, sports, field trips, first steps...those things won't be.

Life happened and I went through a divorce in 2013. It was incredibly tough. But real estate was still there. Real estate helped provide for me and for my boys. As part of being a single mom, I worried about being on a 100% commission job. I prayed about it and decided to take on a job as a paralegal while still running my brokerage. Law had always been a big interest to me, but rather than put myself through years of law school and lots of debt doing so, I obtained my paralegal certificate at SMU and worked for a law firm. That didn't last long, because I wasn't staying true to my passion of being there for my kids like I wanted to. God and I had lots of conversations and so one Sunday, I woke up and felt Him telling me to go to church that day. I hadn't been in a while, but I couldn't ignore this push to go to church that exact day. So I did - and it changed my life. When I walked in the gentleman handing out church programs stopped me. He explained that he was a headhunter and had recognized me from my photo on LinkedIn. He went on to say that he was going to be calling me that week to see if I was interested in taking a job closer to my house, paying way more than I was making. I couldn't believe the twist of fate that day. I sat through the church service crying and ended up not only taking the interview but accepting a job with the company that would end up being my brokerage investor partner! I was able to run my brokerage from their office while also assisting companies find commercial real estate space, relocate employees, manage a small portfolio of rental properties and learn from a serial entrepreneur - it was a huge blessing in my life to this day. They believed in what I was doing in my real estate business and decided to help me rebrand my brokerage. In March 2019, we took a small office that had just a handful of agents, and over the next two-and-a-half years, grew it to an office of over 60 agents!

Q: Wow, that is incredible.
KD: Yes. During that same time more blessings flowed my way. I reunited with a friend of mine from high school. He had his real estate license and half joking, I told him he needed to come work for me! Long story short, he did, and now we're married. So my husband's a realtor too; it's 24/7 real estate in our house!

When I look back at some of the obstacles I had to go through, I remember that being a broker at the age of

30 was tough. I got a lot of looks from some agents saying I was too young to be a broker. I had to overcome a lot of mindset issues. I found myself asking, can I do this? I wasn't the number-one agent in Dallas. Why do I think I should open my own brokerage? Why do I think I have a leg to stand on here?

And really, it just kept coming back to my belief that those things don't matter. It's family first! I reminded myself, you're doing this for your family. My definition of success doesn't need to look like the woman next to me. As long as I was doing it with integrity and the way that I love doing it and I provided for my family, that's all that matters. And to this day, that's still the premise behind our Simply Texas Real Estate manifesto.

Q: I love this story. I love it because there are a lot of things that you're sharing that I think that people can pick up on. Number one, you are very clear about putting family first. You probably even treat your team, even if they're not really your family, they're probably now your family because to you that's kind of your thing and how you grow.

KD: Yes. When my sister and I started in business, our first tagline was "Real Family Real Estate". Today any new agent that joins us gets a welcome box with a welcome gift, they're recognized, and then they create a business plan with me that corresponds to their goals. It's very personalized.

Q: Yes. What advice would you give to a woman who wants to jump in and maybe join your team or just get started in real estate. Because many people wonder if they can do it, are they good enough, do they know enough, all those things. And I want to say one thing before you answer. This is in every industry. Anyone can have those limiting beliefs, or that "itty bitty shitty committee" that we all have that's doubting our abilities. What would you say to her?

KD: I firmly believe that any woman can get started in real estate and be successful. And I think even more so in the day and age that we live in, as opposed to 20 or 30 years ago. The way we do our job has completely changed with the advancement of technology. My grandmother was in real estate back in the seventies and eighties. I remember talking to her about it and just how different it looked back then. I'm so appreciative of the conveniences we have now. When I look at the impact that technology and social media has had on my life - and the fact that it's all at our fingertips, we can truly do this job from anywhere.

And so it all comes down to your mindset, your hustle, and your priorities. You know, I can teach you to do a contract, but if you don't have the drive to get out of bed every day and to put a schedule together and to have your priorities in check, then I don't know what to tell you. But if you do have those things, if you have the drive, then anyone can be successful. Even with kids, because kids have a certain ebb and flow to their schedule. So it might mean for a couple of years, you wake up early before they're up and you knock out some work. And then when they're napping, you get a little bit more done, or maybe you're a night owl and you stay up and you do a little bit more, but you can do it. You just have to get creative.

And that is a beautiful thing. My grandmother didn't have that luxury years ago. And I think that if you can do that, even if it means you're providing 4, 6, or 8 transactions a year for your family, then by the time your kids are in high school and say, "Mom, I'm going out with my friends," now you've found yourself with a lot more time on your hands. Then guess what? Now you can hit it hard. And now you have repeat clients. Now you've got people who know you, like you and trust you! By then your brand has been established. Imagine if they had waited like many women do. The median age of a Realtor is 56…imagine the years they could've been building their business and laying the foundation.

Moms of young kids are so relatable! Who are you going to trust with your family's biggest decision? Women are a natural choice to serve as agents. We are the heart of the family. We know exactly how buying this particular house is going to affect each member of our family. And I think that that makes us more relevant. You know the whole, "know, like, and trust" factor, when you're trying to attract people to work with you? You've got it. You're naturally in all of these different circles, whether it be your kids' sports, clubs or PTA. Moms just naturally will find themselves surrounded by people. The most successful Realtors are the ones that are social and have a lot of those connections.

So if you can learn to be a great connector with people and you have some hustle and drive, then you can be fantastic at this business; all day long, you should do this. You have the ability to make as much as you want - you'll get out of it what you put into it.

Q: So true. What inspires you now? Because initially it probably inspired you to work for your kids, put a roof over their heads and other things. Now you've been in this a while, you've got over 50 agents, you're still finding that drive. What inspires that?

KD: I truly found a love for helping other people succeed in the business and feel it's my calling. Now it's not just the joy of helping people buy or sell a home. I now get to do both! My husband and I divide up our workload, so he spends most of his time with our personal clients, which leaves me to do what I really love. And that is helping women get a foothold in this industry, while still being an active mom in their homes and laying the foundation of their business earlier than most. What keeps me going every day is celebrating their successes while building a legacy for my family. At the end of the day, if you wake up and you've sold a million houses, but yet your kids don't know who you are because they never see you, and you haven't taken the time to create memories with them, what is it all worth? That's really the passion that drives me. To drive that point home even further, we just experienced a scare last year when my husband was diagnosed with cancer. It hit us hard out of left field. Nothing like a diagnosis like that to make you evaluate your priorities in life. It was that turn of events that caused me to look into the EXP platform last year. You never know what God's going to put in your path to force you to pivot. Moving to EXP allowed me to shed the parts of being a broker/owner that distracted me from doing what I loved - while adding extra income streams to not just my business but all of my agent's businesses - while also helping each and every one of us save for retirement. So to answer your question, it really comes down to my faith that continues to inspire and drive me. Time and time again God has put difficult situations in my path - and each time I feel it has brought me closer to fulfilling God's purpose for my life.

Q: I appreciate your story. I appreciate that you are showing that it's possible, especially for a woman, especially for someone who went to college for something completely different, to find what you're great at and go for it. You know what's funny, Kim, just yesterday I was talking to my cousin. He's young. He's not sure what he needs to do. He has hustle in him. He has a sales drive in him. And he said to us, you know, I'm thinking maybe I should go into real estate. I'm like, yes.

KD: Absolutely. Just this year, I've helped several women kick start their real estate business who are in their early twenties with little ones at home just like I was. It makes me smile knowing that they've seen the light and have begun to build their legacy.

Q: Amazing. Do you have agents all over the U.S.? Do you specifically have agents to work for? I know real estate has changed so much and because of the way EXP works, it seems like it's possible for you to have agents everywhere.

KD: It is now. And that's one of the many reasons we decided to align with EXP Realty last year. We moved our boutique brokerage to the EXP platform in October of 2021 with agents all over the Dallas- Fort Worth Metroplex. If you know DFW, it's more than 200 different cities and towns, so it feels like it's our own little country anyway. So we have Texas, but by joining the EXP network we recently opened up Simply Illinois. One of our agents opened up that brand and she's growing her business and our way of doing real estate in Illinois. She's spreading the same philosophies, the same beliefs that we have about how you should treat your clients and each other. We also launched the Simply Oklahoma brand with my sister after she became dually licensed. I would love to be able to spread our "Simply" brand to all 50 states and other countries. And I'm having so much fun with it and being able to see people's lives changed through this model. Whereas before it only benefited a broker or team leader to run a team like this. Now, any agent within EXP can have the same opportunity to grow throughout the country. I love that level playing field that it provides everyone.

Q: It's amazing Kim, where can someone find you, and find out more about your team? Or maybe they just want to ask a question because something that you said sparked something in them.

KD: Yes! You can find me on Instagram or TikTok @ SimplyKimDean. You can find me, Kim Dean, on Facebook. My group at EXP is the Simply Texas Real Estate Group. You can find that group on Instagram and Facebook. And our website is www.GoSimplyTexas.com.

Q: I cannot wait for all the great stuff that we're doing this year. Thank you so much for taking your time to hang out with me, Kim.

KD: Thank you. It was a lot of fun.

KIM DEAN

www.GoSimplyTexas.com

Kim Dean has been in Texas real estate since 2003. Aside from a brief time as a pharmaceutical sales rep, real estate is all she's known since graduating from Texas A&M with a degree in Agribusiness and Speech Communications.

After working for a homebuilder and 2 large franchises, Kim became an independent boutique brokerage owner partnering with her sister in late 2008. Putting her faith and family first has always been the driving force behind her business values and her company manifesto.

After a season of life changes, Kim re-branded her brokerage as Simply Texas Real Estate in March of 2019 and grew it to an office of over 60 agents before partnering with eXp Realty in October of 2021. Her team sold in excess of $140M in 2021 and grew 100% organically by creating a family culture and an environment filled with collaboration and the belief that everyone can create their own version of success in real estate. She has a passion to help women begin a career in real estate at ANY age, to help reduce the failure rate in the industry, and to spread the "Simply" branding and culture to all 50 states!

Kim and her agent husband Derek have received D Magazine's Best of Dallas awards and in February 2021 received the award for #1 agent in McKinney TX on social media by PropertySpark.

She is the mom of two boys (ages 14 and 20) and one furbaby - a golden retriever named Aspen. She and Derek love to travel, visit wineries, watch their youngest play travel hockey and visit their oldest son in Maine where he attends college.

KATHY HELBIG-STRICK
Experience Real Estate Partners
with EXP, CEO

CHAPTER 5

Giving People a Platform to be Successful

with Kathy Helbig-Strick

HEY THERE, SUPERWOMEN. I AM SO EXCITED TO have my next guest. I'm excited every time I talk to a boss lady anyway, but when I talk to one who's in an industry that I'm familiar with, I love it. I was in real estate for 21 years, on both the residential and the commercial sides. But this woman has really created an amazing career in the real estate industry, including being a broker. It's amazing what she's created, having teams before there were teams. There's so much richness to her story. I am super excited to have her on the show.

Q: Kathy Helbig-Strick, how are you?
Kathy Helbig-Strick: I'm fantastic. Thank you so much for having me.

Q: I'm excited to talk to you. You're from St. Louis, right?
KS: Yes ma'am. Born and raised my whole life in St. Louis, Missouri.

Q: You've been a full-time realtor for 26 years. You're currently a broker and you have had one of the highest-selling teams over the last 23 years. That's crazy.
KS: Yes. It's been quite a ride, for sure.

Q: So there are a lot of questions I want to ask, not just about women in real estate because your story does relate to a lot of things. It's about a lot of reasons that women go through, why we make the decisions we have to make, how to raise kids, and also be a boss—figuring all that out.
KS: I'm still figuring it out every single day.

Q: Like all of us, right?
KS: That's right.

Q: Let's start with how you got into real estate. Tell me how that came about.
KS: Sure. I was a young newlywed in my early twenties, not expecting to get pregnant just four months after I got married. I was in outside sales at the time, but the travel and physical demands of that job didn't mix well with having a newborn! So after having my son, Brandon, I stayed home with him for his first two years, then soon would be

expecting again, our second child, my daughter Kaila. After 2 years out of the workforce, I decided at that point that I needed something outside the home to keep me stimulated and just bring in a little bit of extra income during those days. So, I happened to run across a small-time broker who was advertising on the radio for a real estate seminar, back in the day before people were doing that kind of thing. Long story short, he said, "You should really be in real estate. If I sponsor your licensing, will you come work for me? You can work part-time and make a whole lot of money." So I was like, "I'm in!" I jumped into real estate school, got my license, and worked for him. I only lasted about a month there, because I was quickly discovering that I was not a great fit and was realizing that maybe he wasn't as truthful as he should have been, especially about how "easy" real estate would be and the time commitment it would require to make a whole lot of money.

Then, it was recommended to me that I talk to another broker, so I went over to the largest independent brokerage in town at the time and started immediately. It was an interesting time in real estate, as this was 1997 and just before the Internet and real estate played together. So, I jumped over to my new brokerage and my part-time days were pretty much over within a couple of months. Business took off, fast. I loved it. It got into my blood, deep. Then baby number two made her debut, and so basically, I'm juggling files on my head, a toddler in my hand, and a newborn on my hip most days, just flying in and out of the office to keep up. A lot of people seemed baffled at my sudden success as they kept asking me, "What on earth are you doing girl? How are you so busy so fast!" I didn't know any difference, I thought this was pretty normal, so

I was like, "I don't really know! I don't even know what I'm doing yet, I'm just trying to keep up." Back then there wasn't really much training for agents, and training on how to run a real estate business was non-existent. Once you got licensed, it was pretty much like, hey congratulations, you passed your test! And it was sink or swim time. You were turned loose to figure it out and basically learned from your clients along the way, praying you didn't mess anything up too bad! You did the usual realtor stuff. You know, sign up for phone duty shifts, go do a bunch of open houses, and then with a pat on the back and a good luck kid, you're in business! And that's kind of how it worked. So, I was fortunate enough to have gotten real busy, real fast, and by year two, decided there has got to be a better way than trying to do everything myself!

Q: That's incredible. First of all, good for you for just jumping in and doing something and going for it. There must have been some kind of magic about you or something that you were doing to attract the clients. What do you think it was back then when you were just starting?

KS: It's funny that you say that because I'm born and raised in St. Louis and anybody that knows anything about real estate knows that the fast track to success is usually through your network, right? Well, even though I was a local all my life, I didn't have much of a network. My background is really kind of interesting, and not what most people who know me would think. I was raised in a very sheltered, very Christian family environment. From 1st grade through 8th grade, I went to a Baptist one-room schoolhouse, though we weren't Baptist, so I didn't necessarily really fit in there perfectly, the beginning of a trend ha! Our school was part of a church that was converted to a school and there were only maybe 10 people around my grade at that point. The curriculum was unique, much like homeschooling, we all worked at our own pace in our individual small cubicles they called "offices". It was a far cry from the traditional open classroom setting nor did we move around to different classrooms interfacing with different friend groups. We would set our weekly goals with the lead teacher every Monday, then worked at our own pace to achieve those goals each week and were rewarded with certain privileges when we met or succeeded those goals. Looking back, that experience instilled some great habits in me. By the time I reached high school age, my parents had found a new church across town and moved me to that Christian high school as a freshman. But that school wasn't much bigger, it had a graduating class of 12 people! So again, not building much of a network yet!

Although I gained a lot of good structure, not being in the mainstream or the traditional school systems definitely limited my exposure as compared to most people, therefore limiting my relationships. In addition, the St. Louis area is predominantly Catholic, so the parish schools as well as some large private schools were prevalent. Those schools were very sought after, well attended, and tight knit! In addition, St. Louis is very geographically divided. So where you are from and the schools you attended says a lot about your social or economic class. In St. Louis, (and this is definitely a known St. Louis thing!) When people ask each other "where did you go to school" they aren't referring to what college, they mean what High School, since that is typically the indicator of your background and in a lot of cases hinted at your economic stature. So being from "the right" part of town or in the right schools early on can be very advantageous as people are starting to form communities and make networks from an early age. Clearly, I had neither going for me…I've always been like a little salmon swimming up-steam even from early childhood! And unlike most graduates who went on to college, and made even more connections there, I unfortunately did not. Although we were just an hour and a half away from The University of Missouri, Columbia or, better known as Mizzou, which is a very big Missouri University, my parents never really even talked to me about pursuing college as an option. Even though I was a straight A student, I guess it was never a thing in our house, maybe because my mom was a stay-at-home mom, and only 1 of my 3 other siblings pursued college, so they just didn't encourage it for me. Don't get me wrong, I had the best, most supportive parents in the world…but I was the last of four kids, and my parents were 42 when they had me. In addition, they were also dealing with some pretty heavy family trauma throughout most of my early childhood years. My poor mother lived at church to be able to deal with it all, and my father had to work all the time to support the family, so it was kind of like they were there, but not all there for many of those formative years. My oldest siblings were 16 (brother) and 14 (sister) years older than me, then came my closest brother who was 4 years older. We were literally like 2 different generations with the age differences. Then the family dynamics changed again when I was around 11, when we had my oldest brother who I hadn't seen since I was 3, along with 2 of his children, my niece and nephew who were 5 and 2 moved in with us for 5 years. Supposedly your birth order has a lot to do with your personality traits that you end up getting, but with that time in my life topsy-turvy, I'm more of a mutt I suppose as I kind of fell into two categories as this turn of events changed everything. We now had 2 new babies of the household, and an adult brother home I really didn't remember knowing.

I finished high school early, but never ended up pursuing college. I worked a full-time job ever since I was 17 and had been in a relationship for 4 years. So, my plan all through high school had been to get married to my high school sweetheart and have babies some day! It sure seemed like I was on my way to that plan as at barely 19 years old we got engaged. But some circumstances changed with those future plans, and we didn't end up getting married; we called off the engagement half-way through planning a wedding and decided to stay friends.

With this change of plans, I ventured out on my own, moved out at 19, and I had to figure out what was next for me. I had no career aspirations since marriage and raising kids had been my only plans until now, so I was a little lost. But that old boyfriend, who was a car enthusiast, suggested I try to get a job in car sales.

So here I am 19, with a babyface that had me looking more like 14—and car sales was NOT in my comfort zone, but I needed a job and was up for any challenge. He found a help wanted ad at the new Acura dealership on the opposite side of town and he pushed me to go check it out.

Acura was a new luxury line that had recently hit the market, so it was a more upscale place. From what I could tell, it was an all-male salesforce that I was walking into. Auto sales was pretty much an all-male industry, period, at that time. "Here goes nothing", I thought! So I applied, had a quick interview with the manager, and to my surprise I was hired! I had a sneaking suspicion from the snickering and whispers while I was there, that I was probably really hired mostly as a joke, but I was ready to give it my all regardless!

So I did just that! After I proved myself, some of the guys did tell me later that I was hired as a dare and that they were laughing about me boldly walking in in my heels and saying, "Excuse me, I'd like to apply for a job to sell cars." But that's exactly what I did, and to my surprise they gave me the job and a short leash to see what I could do. I don't think anyone expected me to do anything but to fall on my face, but I didn't, and after the first couple of months I was holding my own and was almost always at the top of the sales board.

But here's what was interesting; I was succeeding at something that I knew nothing about. I wasn't the most experienced one on the showroom floor, I knew nothing about cars actually, but I did know how to connect with people, how to work hard, set goals and be self-motivated. I also think my innocence and honesty was non-threatening to my customers and was probably what made people come back to me. Dealing with me was a different experience, and although I may have not been *THE MOST* knowledgeable, they liked dealing with me. I mean who didn't usually dread the car buying experience back then with all the high-pressured sales tactic and games you had to play! But I wasn't that typical salesperson, and I had no game! So those customers that I talked with who were still just gathering information, came back and asked for me, because they wanted to buy from me! So being different, and empathetic, and more relational versus high pressure and salesy, made me stand out. I excelled in auto sales for the next 3 years honing those sales and relationship-building skills. And although that wasn't the traditional route of a 19-year-old girl, and though I do have regrets of missing out on college, I am so grateful for that opportunity. Those skills along with my early development habits, really set me up for success and easily translated into the building blocks for my future real estate business as well.

Q: Really?

KS: Yes, fast forward about 7 years from there, I was still trying to find my place in life and was regrouping after a failed, very brief marriage that I jumped into at 22 years old, to a competing auto dealer's son while I was still in the car business. Post divorce, I was now enjoying an outside sales job, still revolving around the auto business. I re-married at 26, that time was not so brief. We were together for almost 25 years and brought 3 wonderful kids into the world.

And this is where we pick back up to the start of my real estate career. Circa 1997, online real estate or social media was not a thing yet. I built my business pretty much on forming fast relationships and gaining as much knowledge about real estate that I could. I was always forward thinking and went out of my way to get educated. I was great at interacting at open houses and farming in those early days. I did the ice cream truck rounds every summer to my farm neighborhoods. I did the garage sales. I knocked on doors to meet people. I wrote monthly neighborhood newsletters. I even created a website for my farm neighborhoods called WhatDidTheyGetForIt.com so everyone could see what homes in the area were selling for right after closing, since Zillow wasn't a thing yet. Back then, you'd have to wait months for the county records to be updated to see what homes sold for if you weren't a realtor with MLS access. Then once the internet did come into play, I was an early adopter and ran with internet marketing, full force while a lot of others were in denial of what was coming to our industry, that would turn traditional real estate on its head!

Marketing and branding around real estate became a thrill and passion of mine, so I really excelled there!

Q: You were just hustling. You were out there and not giving up. I love that you went into sales first. You and I are probably around the same age. In our generation, sales were kind of one of those words that we didn't like to hear. A lot of women were scared of sales. But it's really good that you went in and got that skill first, along with relationship-building.

KS: Yes, and I'm especially grateful that it was car sales. That was a learning opportunity on so many levels. Talk about learning how to overcome obstacles and in addition, experiencing and overcoming all the "Me Too" challenges along the way. Back then it was rampant! I dealt with all kinds of sexual harassment, outright groping, and inappropriate sexual advances on a daily basis, but I was young and naïve and thought that was just part of life as a woman, so I dealt with it, and just tried to figure out how to use being a woman to my advantage in spite of all of that. Those were crazy times back then; I could tell you some stories of some of the things I had to endure. It's sad, now that I know better. But those situations made me tough. Looking back, it definitely toughened me up!

Q: I would bet. This brings us to some of the difficulties of building a business. You've been in real estate for a long time, you've seen some ups and downs. Being a boss lady is not easy, that's for sure. So tell me some of the things that you've had to deal with in your life and in your business.

KS: I'd say some of the hardest things to deal with started with just trying to fit in and climb the ladder in the industry.

I was always looking to stay ahead of the curve in my career, and so that meant getting out of St. Louis as often as I could to seek out knowledge and trends before they'd ever hit our market. In doing that, I often attended conferences, masterminds, and conventions alone. Sadly, being alone and a woman in those environments can prove to be very tricky! You're trying to make connections, and to do so you need to get yourself into the right rooms with the right people. So, you would have to go to the mixers, the sponsored happy hours, set up "lobby-con" meetings with complete strangers and just be out there mingling. For me, that alone was stressful being that I was pretty introverted. But in addition, for many many years, those gatherings were predominately attended by the males in the industry. So it proved to be particularly challenging to try to make connections in that environment without being hit on, propositioned, or even worse than that on a few occasions. I had to become a master at handling those situations without alienating myself from circles. It was so hard to be just friendly enough to be included, without inviting unwanted attention. Sadly, that was a recurring issue that I believe held me back, until I started bringing my husband along. Now we do all events together and I don't hesitate to walk into a room!

Another challenge I wasn't prepared for was how so many people hate on and judge successful women rather than celebrate them. A successful man is considered a BEAST.... but a successful woman is often assumed to be a different "B" word. And other women tend to be the worst offenders. I can't tell you how many times I have heard people making (inaccurate) assumptions about me who have never even met me. But even worse, the secret judgment from friends and family can be devastating. I experienced some pretty serious mom shaming by a very close friend who was secretly judging me and undermining me to my children for years. She was a stay-at-home mom and believed since I chose to be a mom AND have a career, that made me a bad mom. Mom shaming is a terrible thing…we all have our own roads in life so ladies we need to support each other even if their choices are different than ours. I may be biased but I think my kids turned out to be pretty freaking amazing kids, praise the lord! And women CAN have it both ways! It's more than OK to forge your own path.

Lastly, the challenge of scaling in real estate has been an ongoing challenge. When it was all about ME, MY sales, MY actions, the success and income was determined by me. I controlled my destiny, right? I controlled my income. How hard I worked and how many houses I closed equated to what I was going to make that year. And I was making great money being a solo real estate agent, but I was also reaching capacity. So I started a team to help me scale, really before teams were a model. I had no one to lead the way, if I recall I think there were one or two other agents starting teams at that time too, but I really hadn't heard about them yet, we were emerging around the same time. So with no one to learn from, it was all trial and error at that time. And boy were there lots of "errors" along the way. When I got into real estate, it was a solo sport for the most part…you'd see the occasional husband-and-wife teams, but there were no multi-agent teams to speak of. Agents had to be the jack of all trades, salesperson, marketer, admin, tech, advertising specialist and more! And when you ran out of time, your income was capped. Well, I was running out of time by year two! Luckily, I recognized the potential lost revenue with the overflow I couldn't handle properly, and I decided to try bringing in other agents to help with that overflow. I started a team in just my second year in the business, it took some adjusting over the years but bringing in others was necessary to grow. I looked at it this way, I'd rather capture some of that revenue than none of it from being over extended, so it's certainly worth trying! Looking back, I guess you could say I was a true pioneer in our area with building a team model. I'm proud of that as it wasn't an easy road to navigate. Team models weren't yet supported by the brokerages, and there was always the challenge of finding the right people to grow with! I definitely failed forward a lot over the years, but also achieved some pretty impressive milestones.

One of my first mistakes was the idea to partner instead of forming a team under me. And in addition, we entered this partnership based on the old hey I like you, and there's a need to fill, so let's all partner, method! That was the extent of how much thought went into it. A lunch was set with a mother/daughter in my brokerage who seemed friendly and competent, and we emerged with a handshake deal. That partnership sadly ended in a lawsuit between us when I wanted to part ways with them 3 years later. So that was a really big learning experience, and so heartbreaking. Once we settled our exit from each other, I just started over. At that point I said to myself, "I've learned the hard way, there can't be three cooks in the kitchen, there has to be a leader this time around and since I'm passionate and very particular about how I want my business to look, that leader needs to be me." My partners weren't bad people, we just went into things unprepared and three strong minded women trying to be equal partners, was just a recipe for disaster. And so I just burned it down and rebuilt it as a team and then put my head down and just sold the heck out of houses for the next several years! And I loved it. I was fine-tuning a small team and in no time, we became the highest-selling team in the Missouri region. But I was growing a little tired keeping up with the volume we were selling, learning to manage people, as well as trying to be a good mom to two toddlers, and now after a seven-year gap later, added our third baby Alaina to the equation! It was now 2007 and I had my entire team just humming and working from my basement and life was good! Busy, but good!

Then about that time, I had an opportunity presented to me. I was being sought after and offered ownership of a newer brokerage in town. This brokerage/franchise was relatively new in St. Louis, not at all a well-known name yet. With their model, they looked for successful agents who had a good reputation and lots of market share to invest in their franchises and anchor their launches. I was excited by the new opportunity and thrilled that after much vetting, they offered me, and a small partnership group the opportunity to open up a franchise. Until these conversations, I really had never envisioned such an opportunity. I loved the idea of taking what I had learned over the years to a whole new level. Plus selling at the level we were selling was exhausting. Who knew there was more opportunity than selling houses in the real estate business! They wanted me to coach, they wanted me to be a connector in the area and help them grow more market centers quickly, and still keep my sales team in play! That was really the first time I had ever thought about doing something related to real estate, aside from selling houses and I was getting kind of excited at the prospect! After so many months of saying no, I finally said yes. My eyes had been opened to all kinds of new possibilities, so I took the risk, I jumped in with a few other partners and we brought in the first franchise for that brand in St. Charles County.

Oh, I must mention this was late 2007, early 2008 when we decided to open a franchise in real estate. We were launching when real estate was crumbling, what were we thinking?

Of course, everyone's sales were plummeting then, but despite that and a lot of turmoil behind the scenes, we managed to build this incredible office and market center over the next nine years. And it was one of the top-producing offices in the area, but unfortunately it was a very tumultuous experience and ultimately was not the right fit for me.

This time in my life I faced a lot of adversity and learned that what's on the surface isn't always what you get, and "leaders" aren't always good people to follow. This is a bit of a touchy subject for me, so let me tread lightly here as I have nothing against my former company as a whole; I know there were a lot of good people there, still to this day. But a good company can make mistakes when scaling and elevating the wrong people can turn the culture on a dime and leave collateral damage. And that's exactly what I was experiencing, it all turned on a dime. What started out good was now toxic for me.

It was unfortunate that I was one of several of the early casualties that came out of this new leader who was rising rapidly within the company but had prioritized personal agendas and greed above the culture I had been drawn to initially. I was shell-shocked by the overnight change in things and by the bullying that was taking place! At first, I thought it was just happening to me, but then it started to come out that several other good people were also encountering some of the same situations behind the scenes. I wasn't quite sure what to do, none of us did. I felt helpless.

In addition, our local partnership group was falling apart at the seams just months after launching, and over time we were being pitted against each other. What no one knew at the time, was we were being manipulated and bullied by the person we trusted and had admired at the time we all made the decisions to do this together. Most of the partners had bailed out at this time and I was left with trying to figure out what had gone so wrong, so fast! There was something going on behind the scenes, an agenda being hatched, and this girl was not going to just accept it or play along into what was happening. So, I started to speak up about the injustices and tried to hold strong. But out of retaliation, I was basically put on an island so that I wouldn't be "the fly in the ointment" with all that I knew and had been experiencing behind the curtain. I often describe the experience, at the level I was at, like when Dorothy saw the real OZ behind the screen. It was so disappointing maneuvering through all the politics and smoke and mirrors. The sexist behavior in play was sickening and I experienced and witnessed an overwhelming amount of bullying and intimidation tactics during that time, it was simply shocking. There were a lot of anti-women agenda's behind the scenes in play that people didn't realize. Great agents and leaders were being discarded left and right all in the name of "culture" and the growth initiatives. It felt like there was this overnight shift that had become about the growth, at any cost, and it was heart-breaking. And I just couldn't buy into that or recruit to that. I didn't wish it on my worst enemy much less my peers. Instead, I pushed back and tried to stand against what was happening, trying to find someone to listen and do something about it. But I was up against the person who was the rising star and not only over our entire region, but also moving up the ranks quickly to soon be over the entire company. I wasn't going to cave to the bullying and intimidation and just be one of the yes people because that's what you had to do to move ahead.

And so of course that caused a conflict, a huge one, and a behind the scenes battle was waging. Now I find myself in a company where I'm part owner but suddenly instead of the "darling", I'm an outcast. I was painted as difficult and not a fit for "the culture", his culture that is. But I didn't sign up for THAT culture, that was ugly and vile, but no one believed that what was happening to me, could really be happening. So, for the first time in my life, I was doubted, and I felt alone, and just like that, I felt this glass ceiling come over me, a real hopelessness. I was not only working, but I was an owner of an organization that wanted to put me on an island, assassinate my character and silence me. I was faced with the reality that under those circumstances I couldn't succeed there. That was really, really tough for me to deal with. It actually put me into a depression. I barely went into the office for a year. It was hard for me to leave the house. I let my team just go on autopilot some weeks while I was dealing with all the emotional trauma and battles behind the scenes. Here we are in a real estate market, our sales were down about 15% from the prior year since homeowners were in a world of hurt, yet my small team still managed to stay in the top 5 for highest sales even with my head space a mess at times. By anyone's measure we were doing great during that time, and my team was #1 in our office and #2 in the area at the company, but as a tactic to try to break me, we were called out for the slump in our sales and thrown off from their agent leadership council. I received an email saying since my sales volume had dropped, I was being removed so I could focus on my sales since they said "it looked bad for recruiting purposes". For perspective, my sales were triple if not quadruple most of the others on the leadership council. Man those were some tough days! They were trying hard to get me to walk away…and some days I was so close to doing just that.

It was all so demoralizing to the point I was contemplating leaving the real estate business entirely because I was so broken from the experience. But something in me just couldn't roll up in a little ball like I wanted to. So with the help of my supportive team, I pulled myself up by the bootstraps, made a plan and came out from the fog of that despair. I wasn't going to let that adversity sideline me any longer, instead we would turn all the negative energy into the fuel and drive we needed to propel us forward and break through. I would just need to write this decade off as another major learning experience.

So it's decided, it's time to go. But, what I wasn't prepared for, was it wasn't that easy to just pick up and move. Unlike any regular real estate agent, as an owner in a franchise, you can't just leave and go sell houses somewhere else tomorrow. You're in breach of your obligations as an owner if you move your license, and you certainly can't just open a competing company. So I was held at a standstill for 5 years in a vicious circle trying to untangle and get my freedom to leave.

During those years, almost every brand in town was trying to get me to open with them. But at that point in time, I was still being held hostage in my partnership. And I just wasn't feeling a strong enough fit with anyone to jump back into a franchise once I was free. I had to do some heavy soul searching. I knew I wasn't feeling ready to try to anchor another brand new to the area. I came to the realization that I was feeling so broken at that time, that I needed time to heal. Going to another brokerage was the last thing that appealed to me. All that time I was pretty much suffering in silence and although I still had a great reputation for real estate and for sales in the area, I didn't have the wherewithal to go help someone else build their brand and be at the mercy of another franchise agreement. And honestly, I didn't know for a certainty if I was even staying in the business much longer. Sad that here I was in the top 10 out of 15,000 real estate agents, sought-after by many brands yet I was thinking about walking away from it all entirely.

Q: It's so tough for women. I know it's tough for a lot of people, but for women, we do have an extra layer or two or ten that we have to navigate through. You got to a really low place, so what was the thing that made you say, "Okay, Kathy, people are depending on you" or "You're better than this" or what was the thing that said, "You can do it, get up"?

KS: I think it was my stubbornness. Once I saw a little bit of light, I managed to get out from under that dark cloud of depression I had been wrestling with, and feeling like a failure for those years literally not knowing how to handle it all. This was all new to me. Yes, I had some learning opportunities along the way, but for the most part I always figured out the obstacles, and success came pretty easily to me before all of this. I was always a leader in almost everything that I did, and then suddenly I'm feeling like

I'm failing at something and almost failing publicly! Here I was the girl all over the billboards, the TV and radio, the girl that's selling all the houses, the girl that got an opportunity to now be an owner of a franchise and I'm repping for all the ladies because usually it was mostly just the men that are in the high levels in real estate positions.

And I was very proud of that, in the beginning, and then I was really, really disappointed, and then a little bit ashamed that I couldn't turn it around, no matter what I did. And believe me I tried every possible work around. It just wasn't working, I had no one to go to for resolution and I couldn't turn it around on my own. I felt so completely beat-down, beat up and so I just kind of retreated. And then finally I almost got to that "f*** it all" place. But then my support system around me kicked my butt and suddenly the fight was back! I was like, "You know what? I'm not going down this way, I'm not letting them win! I'm getting out of here no matter what it takes". It wasn't an easy task and I had to end up paying big attorney fees and settling on my shares value to finally end the insanity. I didn't get what they were worth or what I should have gotten per our written agreements, but it was time to just move on. I agreed to settle out of court to end the madness. Afterall my team had been in this flux with me for years too, I owed it to them to not give up, and lord knows we all needed a fresh start. Also unbeknownst to everyone, I was going through a long breakdown of my marriage during that tumultuous time too, so a fresh start everywhere was in tall order.

Shortly thereafter, I found a new relationship that gave me the added inspiration to put the past behind me and keep going. Little did I know at the time, the guy who was passionately pursuing my loan business, would end up getting more than he bargained for! After just 2 years Steve not only became my #1 loan guy, but he also became my husband and partner. He was undoubtedly my biggest fan. With his love and support along with my 2nd biggest fan and right-hand Kindle, as well as the rest of the team, they were the encouragement I needed to keep pushing through. Daily they would tell me they knew we could do this all on our own…. we basically had been for years anyway. And it really was them who ignited that last little fight in me. We all had come too far and endured too much to just walk away. I owed it to them to turn this negative into a positive!

Q: Oh, man.

KS: So, the decision was made, I decided to go independent at first. I opened my company, Experience Realty Partners, but truth be known, I was a little scared. This town was run mostly by the big brand brokerages. But I knew I had to do this, and the first year we doubled our business, with no brand affiliation. That decision to leave was just what we needed. The cloud was finally off us and there was bright light ahead. My team and I gave a sigh of relief, and we never looked back. We were out from the environment that was holding us back, that was working against me instead of with me. So once we shut all that out, it was like a new awakening and new birth in real estate. And we did really, really well as an independent brokerage growing to the point that I needed to start considering next steps soon.

My passion was not to be a broker-owner. It never was, but it had become necessary in the journey to keep evolving and serving people without all the other distractions. Launching my own company was a way to keep following my passion for helping people and being instrumental in building agents' careers. Little by little we attracted a lot of agents who were at different types of crossroads, both new to the industry and experienced agents seeking systems and support as well as the right mentoring to get to the next level.

My absolute goal for my agents was to guide them and support them in many ways so that they wouldn't have to make some of the mistakes or sacrifices I did or face the adversity I had faced to find success in real estate. I didn't get the opportunity to have a mentor that went before me to learn from. There weren't many women to look up to in my days, and certainly there was no one I knew who knew how to create and manage a team successfully. So I just thought, all right, this must be what I am called to do! I'm going to be that person to bring other women in and help them build a life, a career with renewed excitement and passion through real estate. Because I was encountering a lot of women in their thirties and forties who were at crossroads just like I was, and they were looking for something to get fulfillment from or to increase their income potential. But it's hard to start a new business when you're at that age where you have a myriad of responsibilities, maybe a family to care for, or per- haps you're suddenly the sole supporter without the luxury of a second income to lean on while getting started.

So to jump into a 100% commission industry is really, really hard for some people to do. But the team model opens all kinds of opportunities to get into real estate without all of the risk. I know the challenges, I had them myself, but with this model you can come into real estate without the usual constraints or start up costs. That opened the doors for a lot of people to choose real estate and succeed at it. And although with team models people come and go...but

I know I made a difference to many people along the way, and I'll always be proud of that legacy.

Ok, so now I'm my own brokerage and I've got this team model pretty dialed in, but there were still other industry issues to be tackled. Two big things that I always hated about this industry was the adversity and competition between agents, AND how many consumers feel about and treat agents in general. I wasn't ok with the blatant disrespect I would see people have for our agents or for their time. There is this whole entitlement attitude out there that it's ok for people to use us for our knowledge, take up our time, or have you run them around to show them houses, with no intentions of using you! What other industries do you know of where people are expected to work for free? None. Yet if an agent asks for a commitment so that they can be guaranteed there will eventually be compensation for their expertise and the time they put in, it's met with such negativity. But after deep thought on how we got to this place in public opinion, I realized that the negativity partially exists because so many people have had lackluster, or downright bad real estate experiences. So, I decided early on, that the number one priority for the agents that I turn out, is that they operate in integrity and kindness, and they always strive to deliver an expert experience. We're kind to people, including other agents, period. Not unnecessarily aggressive, arrogant, and not adversarial. You can be a savage negotiator and fight for your client's best interest, but you can still conduct yourself with respect and be kind in the process. This is a non-negotiable for me, and I am proud that we have a stellar reputation with our peers in the business. That's not achieved easily in such a competitive environment.

Now, how do I change public opinion so that our agents don't have to encounter disrespect? I knew the answer, it was going to have to be by changing the consumers EXPERIENCE! I remember the exact situation that triggered this mission. It was a day when a client was being rude to some of my team members. They then reached out to me; they asked me "to send one of my minions over" for whatever they were calling about. That hit me hard. You see it was one thing when I encountered the occasional disrespect, personally but when I saw my team members getting disrespected, or talked down to like that, that was like poking a mama bear! I remember thinking "what kind of people think this is ok, and how did we get here?" Then I took another step back and realized the traditional broker business model created this. There are way too many unqualified agents and the barrier to entry is set just way too low. And so many consumers often end up working with untrained, subpar agents that propels bad attitudes for us all to manage.

Q: Right.

KS: Every time I'd sit down with someone and say, "Tell me about your last real estate experience," they'd be like, "Oh, it was terrible." Almost every single time. So I was like, okay, we got a black eye from ourselves. We punched ourselves in the face with the traditional brokerage models that have never evolved, so our only hope to change the attitude people have developed over the years is to change the experience. Which I set out to do, one person at a time, even if it was going to take me a lifetime. I understood the assignment! But I realized I had to step back further than the customer experience, I had to start with changing the agent experience as they enter the business first. I can't change the experience for the consumer until I can change the experience for the agent, thus training agents to be experts and finding a better real estate model which is what spurred me to make my final move to EXP so that we could be part of an environment that fosters collaboration over competition, and our agents would have actual ownership interest in their company.

Q: What inspires you now, for this next round of agents and this new company that you're now with?
KS: It's still the people that inspire me. It's still about the agents, but honestly, I've gone back into doing a little bit of production again, because I miss that interaction with my sellers! I've always loved working with sellers. I haven't worked with buyers in almost 18 years. I started my team by bringing buyer agents on first to better serve them, and I focused on sellers' needs. It's funny, my husband and I were driving in the car the other day and I had to call a seller and I was going over the stuff with him. I got off the phone and my husband goes, "God, you're so good with sellers, and you love working with them, I can tell from the passion in your voice on that call. It just makes you happy to be helping them". And he was right, it really docs still light my fire to solve people's problems. I know that will never leave me, and I hope I will always continue to impact and inspire other women to be great business women and great humans. And same goes for the men too—we have some pretty incredible men on our team too, I certainly can't overlook them and their place on our team!

More than anything, I want my legacy to be about impact. Impacting people through real estate, whether it be by helping them through a tough transaction or by helping agents launch and grow a rewarding career that they can be proud of, make a good income doing, but also have a balanced life in the process. Although I do feel it's unrealistic to expect perfect balance, because trust me, there are times when things are way out of balance, so you have to be realistic with that buzz word. You do have to establish some boundaries and seek out some balance between all the hard work and hustle it takes to grow a business, or you might find out it just wasn't worth the sacrifice. Seeking to achieve some balance is another driving factor behind perfecting the team model. A well-run team can help each other find some balance through harmony of systems, processes, and holding each other up as well as having each other's backs so that we can step out for a minute if we need to or go on that much needed vacation with your family, without the fear of lost business.

I didn't have that benefit in my early days before I perfected a team. Every time I tried to step out, It wasn't smooth. I'd hand off my file to an agent in the brokerage and try to tell them all the intricacies of the deal or the client, "Oh, hey Susie, can you cover for me next week? Here's da, da, da, da." And then it always went to hell in a handbasket and you're always on the phone anyway the whole time you were trying to get a break. And so that imbalance stole from my family and my marriage and even my friendships when you can't be present even when you're there. So I don't wish that on anybody else in their quest for a successful career in real estate. It's not worth the tradeoff of giving up your family or your relationships. My passion and mission now is to give people a platform to come into this business, be successful, make money, but have a life too, instead of sacrificing it all for a career.

Q: Oh, my goodness, I tell you what, Kathy, you are amazing at what you're doing. I'm so glad that we're working together. If someone wants to connect with you, how would they find you? And what would you suggest they do first if they're excited to get started with your team or in real estate in general?

KS: I'd suggest when it comes to real estate in general, 100% do not try to go into this on your own first. Starting on someone's successful team is the quickest way to get into production and you will learn so much faster. Think about it this way: Most real estate agents average six home sales a year; if you're better than average, you might be selling 10 or 15. Your learning is limited to what you personally experienced during those handful of transactions. But it takes a long time to experience enough different curve balls to reach mastery in real estate! You just can't get to expert level working a few contracts a year.

But when we're pumping several hundred transactions through our 4 walls every single year and the agents are sitting around hearing everything about every deal, their learning is accelerated. The conversations happening every day are priceless learning opportunities! We constantly talk about what's working and what's not. We talk about the contracts that fail, we talk about the contracts that win, the offers that got accepted, and what didn't. We talk strategies and the whole process of building a business daily. And so those agents that come around are learning from hundreds of different transactions every year and learning from someone who has experienced almost every aspect of the real estate business. Most agents won't sell that many homes in their lifetime much less a year. Just imagine how much faster you can become an expert when you get yourself involved with a high producing team! It also helps gives you some instant street cred. Again, going back to our area, I think we have somewhere around 14,000-15,000 agents right now. So you're one of 15,000, what's your value proposition when you're brand new? That's a tough question to answer, because come on, let's face it, you don't have one on your own yet.

But if you can hitch your wagon so to speak, to somebody else that has a reputation for success, and a top performing sales record, then the uncertainty with you being newer becomes a non-issue as you are able to offer the team's value proposition and reputation, while you are yet to establish your own and you're not left to just sink or swim. I don't believe there is any better way to get started or even get better!

Anyone who wants to connect with me can find me online at experience-re.com or follow me on YouTube at The Kathy Helbig Group. Of course, I would love anybody to hit me up on my personal Facebook, where I am under Kathy Helbig-Strick or our business FB at Experience Real Estate Partners, by Kathy Helbig, also follow me on Instagram, where I'm @whatthehelbig, so you can find me there as well as on TikTok, @kathyhelbigstrick. I try to be everywhere!

Q: I love "What the Helbig"!

KS: Full disclosure, I stole that from my daughter Kaila many years ago. I have to give her credit, her friends came up with that when she was in high school. I was just starting to do a lot of radio and social media, so when I heard it, I was like, "oh, wow that's really good… I must have that!" So, I paid her $150 to sell the name to me and we were both happy! But now she's followed me into real estate so I may just have to give that back one day!

Q: I love that. Thank you for being here today.
KS: Yes, absolutely, and thank you. I appreciate the opportunity. I'm really excited to work with all of these amazing ladies and go make some noise in this world together!

KATHY HELBIG-STRICK

Kathy Helbig-Strick has been a full time top producing REALTOR® in the St. Louis and surrounding Counties in MO for 26 years, Throughout Kathy's career, her team has consistently ranked amongst the highest selling teams in the area, most recently ranked by Real Trends at #7 in all of Missouri.

She is and has always been a trailblazer and a well-respected industry leader, establishing one of the first real estate teams in her area over 24 years ago, and was one of the first to embrace the marriage of real estate and technology in the late 90's, propelling her fast rise to success.

Kathy's long list of accolades include being named Businesswoman Of The Year, Realtor Of The Year, Highest Selling Teams in the MO Region, and The Heartland Region, as well as a multi-year Chairman's Club recipient, and achieving the Lifetime Achievement Award in just a few short years. Recently Kathy and her Group were voted Chesterfield's Best Real Estate Company. Kathy is the author of several published articles and published a popular home blog for several years. She is a local radio personality with an 8 year, long-running weekly real estate segment on a popular morning radio show on KTRS. Kathy has also been recognized for her success by the Post-Dispatch and Suburban Journals as one of St. Louis and St. Charles Highest Selling REALTORS® year after year, and St. Louis Magazine has named her as Top in Customer Satisfaction throughout most of her two-decade long sales career.

In 2008, in addition to running her high producing team, Kathy embarked on franchise brokerage ownership as a co/owner, assisting in the debut, launch and growth of the Keller Williams National brand in the St. Charles/West territory for the next 9 years. In 2016, Kathy envisioned something better than "traditional real estate as usual", and she took a leap of faith and launched her own premier boutique-style, independent brokerage, doubling their business in the first year that Experience Realty Partners was established, and has continued driving growth each year for nearly 5 years. That growth and changes in the industry prompted her next steps of merging her Indy brokerage with the fastest growing global real estate company EXP Realty. Kathy continues to coach and mentor agents to enjoy successful real estate careers and serves her agents and clients at the highest levels as a broker/owner, all while maintaining top sales rankings - and is one of 3 highest reviewed agent groups in the St. Louis area with some of the most 5-star reviews!

Kathy, also a licensed MLO along with her husband Steve Strick, a regional Vice President for USA Mortgage, combined their knowledge of the real estate and mortgage industry, as well as their passion for TEAMS, to create a model that provides unique and compliant Mortgage Solutions for the solo agent, broker/owners, and team leaders, that runs parallel to their successful real estate operations. The husband-and-wife duo have helped launched dozens of successful partner branches since 2020 and helped develop a National VA program that gives back thousands to the Veteran community. They are also partners with several of St. Louis' premiere home builders in a successful title company, Arch City Title.

Their expansive knowledge and experience in real estate, mortgage, title, and insurance helps to provide a superior experience and a convenient one-stop solution to better serve their agents and their clients. Her mission has always been to change the real estate experience for the better, one relationship at a time, and she continues to do so by provide the best possible "experience" to both her agents and their customers.

My passion is
to give people a
platform to come
into this business,
be successful, make
money, but have
their life also instead
of sacrificing it for
a career.

—*Kathy Helbig-Strick*

CAROLINE GOSSELIN
Experience NJ Team-EXP Realty
Founder & CEO

CHAPTER 6

Doing Self Care and Listening to your intuition

with Caroline Gosselin

HEY THERE, SUPERWOMEN. I AM REALLY EXCITED to have my next guest. We met a few months ago at an event I was hosting, our book tour in New Jersey. She comes from a real estate background, you guys know how much I love real estate. And she was just a ball of energy. She saw what we were doing, she saw what this project was, and we ended up connecting. And this is one of the things I always say to other women: Look for an opportunity to collaborate and connect with people that are brilliant. And she came up to me and we started talking, and the next thing you know, I think it was a week or two later, we had a whole new project on our hands. So I'm just in awe of this woman because of her tenacity, her ability to turn stuff around fast. Just a minute ago I was telling her that she is one of the only people I've ever met who has been able to execute that way, to get something done, and see it to fruition.

Q: Caroline Gosselin, how are you?
Caroline Gosselin: I'm great, Tam, thank you. You know, I did execute quickly, but quite frankly, I believe it was due to your inspiration and our instant connection! Sometimes you just know you are going to do big things with people.

Q: Yes. And I'm always looking for those kinds of connections, looking for boss ladies to support in any kind of way that I can. When we started talking, I think the wheels started turning right away. I was in real estate for a long time. And you were with this amazing company and I think it just kind of aligned really well. Let's start our conversation with how you got into real estate and what inspired you to build your real estate career this way?
CG: It has been quite a journey getting into the real estate industry, but, in all honesty, that process was haphazard. People are drawn to this field for a variety of reasons and from differing backgrounds. It has always been intriguing to interact with my peers and ask about their path, because you will never hear the same story twice.

I made my way to the east coast of the US after having completed a master's degree in international affairs in Paris, France where I had lived for 4 years. We had just moved to New York City because my husband was starting an MBA program at Columbia University. I started a job as a program

manager with a small non-profit organization that was affiliated with the United Nations. Working in the international
affairs / public relations realm in NYC was an amazing experience. I had the opportunity to travel the country for several
years, working closely with UN Ambassadors, organizing
U.S. Congressional Delegations around important topics
like human trafficking, war refugees and climate issues.

But when we decided to start a family, everything
changed. We moved from Manhattan to the suburbs in
New Jersey. I had my son, I was home with him for about
six months, and then I decided that being a stay-at-home
mom wasn't in the cards for me. I started looking at options
and talking to my family and the idea of going into sales,
particularly real estate sales, came up. And the minute it
did, my ears perked up. The next day I Googled "real estate
licensing class," the following week I was in the class, and
one month later I was licensed and hanging my shingle.

I had moved to New Jersey knowing no one and having zero family in the area, but I was determined. I started
building my sphere of influence in New Jersey, I joined the
local Chamber, the Rotary Club, headed my neighborhood
block-party committee, and joined a women's empowerment
group. The entrepreneurial spirit in me had been awakened.

My first year in real estate, I was working as a solo agent
at a luxury boutique firm. Within a year that firm was bought
out by Coldwell Banker. I stayed with Coldwell Banker for
five years. Toward the end of my time there, I had hired my
first employee - an administrative assistant. Around that
time was when, in the real estate world, the notion of teams
was starting to form. It was a new trend, and I quickly knew
that this was where the industry was headed. It just made
so much sense to me - why should we all be working in our

own little silos when we could come together, collaborate and leverage each other's strengths? I remember a few years in, I caused a stir in the office because I had created an LLC and called it "The Gosselin Group". That was my vision, and I was going to build it. I didn't want to be a solo agent doing everything on my own. I wanted to do the things I was good at and build a team around what I was lacking. I remember the saying, jack of all trades, but master of none - that is how I viewed solo agents doing everything on their own. I remember "the haters" saying, "Who does she think she is calling herself a group?" It is interesting how some people are threatened by ambition. Our office manager at the time, George Kraus, (who to this day I consider one of my best mentors) told me, "Don't listen to them. Just let it slide off you." It wasn't easy, but I did.

Team building was the direction I went in, and I've never looked back. I decided to leave Coldwell Banker and make the move to Sotheby's International Realty, where I spent nearly a decade. My 15 years experience at traditional brokerages boils down to a few observations: The average Realtor has an over-reliance on being spoon fed. They don't take their destiny into their own hands. A huge percentage are there to do it part-time. For those that are doing it full-time, their entrepreneurialism isn't fostered or encouraged - on the contrary. They are content going about their business with blinders on and not being open to a different way (I know, I was one of them!). Their creativity is clamped down with branding guidelines. More importantly, Realtors who work at traditional brokerages have no stake in the company (even those who have spent their entire careers there - they walk away with nothing). None of the Big 5 brands offer ownership or stock to their agents.

Well, the tide is turning now. Just this past year, in January of 2022, I made the bold decision to move our team to EXP Realty - a global firm which I believe is proving itself to be the leader and setting the standard for what the future of real estate will be. The best part is, we, the agents, are shareholders in this new endeavor and have a stake in the outcome. That is a huge paradigm shift.

I watched EXP come on the scene 10 years ago. I had my eye on it. Many of my colleagues in the business were making the move. It caused me to look a little deeper into it. And once you see it, you can't unsee it. It's a whole new model of real estate. It's not even thinking "out of the box" - Glenn Sanford, our founder and CEO, created a whole new box. And this new model is resonating with agents in a massive way because we are growing fast and have over 90K agents across the globe. As Stefan Swanepoel, a leading visionary in our industry with 40 years experience said recently, "there is good, there is great, and then there is EXP."

Transitioning our team to EXP and aligning ourselves with some of the amazing people who have become my business coaches, my mentors, collaborators, and business partners, has been so uplifting. It has removed the veil. We tend to go through life with self-imposed boundaries that come from our upbringing, or what our past employers told us. But as you grow and expand, you can shed these things. You can see that, maybe it doesn't have to work that way. Maybe real estate doesn't have to look like that. I've been truly inspired by the advent of this company and what it's doing to change the lives of people in my world.

When people become "owners", they just think differently. There is also a financial incentive to help your peers built into this model. I have barely been here a year and

I'm blown away by the collaboration and the sharing of ideas. Our business is taking a whole new shape. Being in a collaborative environment is so important.

We attract top agents who value freedom, collaboration and community. Being growth-minded is the common thread with agents making the move. EXP Realty is becoming a global community (and force to be reckoned with!) designed, powered, and owned by agents and we are transforming the real estate experience for agents and consumers.

It's a forward thinking model. We all have a stake in everyone's success. So many things have been born out of the amazing culture of collaboration at EXP. There are amazing agent-centric benefits - tools, training, technology, masterminds, events, and the ability to build ancillary businesses. I don't think there's another company in real estate that benefits and champions the agent as much as EXP does. I truly believe that.

So as you can see, while my team has changed and morphed over the years, we are growing and we will remain a force in the real estate sector here in New Jersey - we just happen to be using the EXP platform to propel us forward and we've never been on more solid ground.

I would say being with the right tribe is of supreme importance, and I've found my tribe here. The women in this very book and our amazing agent partners across the country are my tribe!

Q: I love that. It's amazing, there are a lot of similarities, I think, for women that come into real estate, because it's such an opportunity to build a lifestyle that you need and that you want. If you need to be home and stay with your child, it is an opportunity to do that, because it's really flexible. And then you also were able to build a team that you want and build a lifestyle that you want. Whether you're a single mom or married, it's just a great career. It's versatile, there are so many things you can do. What are some of the challenges that you have dealt with in your life and in your career or in building a team?

CG: Some of the business challenges have been recruiting the right people to our team culture. Agents come into the business quite naively. I don't think HGTV helps our industry, as it creates unrealistic expectations of both agents and consumers of the reality of things. But through education and communication up front, we are able to overcome that.

Finding and implementing the right systems and processes has been a trial and error. I think we've managed to do that. Luckily, I've had an amazing Chief of Operations, Jenna Kelly, who has relentlessly been devoted to making this a priority. We now have checklists, training modules, and support for our agents that are tailor made. Time consuming onboarding processes are now all in one place. Our online "Team Trainual" allows them to go through our comprehensive training at their own pace. Transactions can be chaotic with many moving parts, but now, they live in one place on Monday.com. Communication with our cloud-based team is made easy with Loom videos, Zoom, Slack Huddles, our Team Google Business Drive and Facebook WorkPlace. We also have company wide meetings in the Metaverse. We call this EXP World - a whole business campus which supports

85K+ agents globally through EXP's sister company Virbela. We have truly embraced using technology to up our game and streamline everything for our agents, our operations staff and more importantly our clients!

Just like everyone, I've also encountered some personal obstacles over the years. It's definitely been a journey ... a quest of sorts! Life doesn't really ever go as planned and yes, there are bumps in the road. Shortly after moving to New Jersey and when my son was barely 1, my husband and I divorced. It was not an easy time. Getting divorced really changed the trajectory of what I thought my life would be. I've had to adapt to this new life I've created and sometimes it's exciting, but it can also be very lonely. I have now been a single mom for 15 years and I admit it is one of the hardest things I have ever done. We are forced to be strong and show a brave face for our children and people don't realize how much we are taking on behind closed doors. I have tremendous respect for single mothers - it is extremely hard.

When my marriage came crumbling down, that was a big blow to my confidence. Without going into all the details, when what you thought your life path was going to be gets pulled out from under you - it is very destabilizing. My marriage imploded 6 months post-birth of my son - I was still in that post-partum stupor. My life was turned upside down. That was a pivotal moment in my life. Did I have a little pity party for myself and take some time to lick my wounds? Yes. But I also come from an immigrant family, and you can only do that for so long. I come from a long line of entrepreneurs and risk-takers, and the message was, "Ok, well now get up and keep moving forward."

These pivotal moments that occur over the course of

one's life can turn into life lessons, if you let them. I've experienced heart aches, betrayals from badly vetted business partners, health and financial issues. Quite frankly one of the most humbling of these experiences resulted in my needing to sell my house and downsize with my son. My business was growing, but I had employees and was pouring a lot back into the business. Truth be told, I had no business buying a house as a single mom, but I did it because I thought it would help bring a sense of normalcy to my son growing up. A few years in, I was passing up on needed repairs and realized that I couldn't afford to stay in it. My son still to this day reminds me that he misses that house with his favorite climbing tree in front of it. That sting will always remain.

I have to credit Tara Gilvar, who I met over a decade ago at a local Chamber meeting. She helped me get back on track after my post-divorce stupor. She was creating a grassroots organization - a group of women called B.I.G ("Believe Inspire Grow") in New Jersey. I owe a lot to this organization. I created a chapter in my town where we brought together a group of women entrepreneurs who wanted to collaborate and get together and support each other. This core group of women aided in my success as I worked, raised my son and grew my business over the past decade. They fulfilled my need for support as I was trying to overcome all obstacles and realize my full potential.

My only regret in all that I've experienced is that I wish I had believed in myself and my abilities a little more and sooner. I was so hard on myself. I think if I had given myself a little more grace, I would have been better equipped to weather those storms. But it is life - you must go through the good, the bad, and the ugly.

Last Fall I attended a business mastermind led by Jon Cheplak, an elite performance business coach, in Lake Tahoe. A group of 30 business owners climbed Mount Tallac. It was an amazing experience - it was very symbolic. Hiking up the mountain truly brought home the importance of finding your tribe and your stride. Coming down that mountain I had a lot more clarity of where I wanted to take my life and business. Getting out of the day to day and giving yourself space to think about your intentions and goals is so crucial. Doing it in the company of others in your field who are performing at a much higher level than you is life changing.

I was moved to create a community for Realtors called "In Quest of Better". I created it because I wanted to bring agents who want to take a holistic approach to their journey together. I truly believe that outward change comes after we've made changes within. It's not just about being on the quest for a better business, always trying to grow clients and be more efficient and scale - but it's also about the quest for a better life. They're interconnected in so many ways. For me, it's been a journey, trying to get through my business ups and downs and my life ups and downs, and trying to take it in stride as it comes and learn from it. I wanted to create a forum and community to help both new agents and seasoned agents navigate those tough waters - together and learn and support each other. We have a Facebook group called "In Quest of Better" and we also have created "The Quest Conference" to bring together these ideas. The inaugural event which will be taking place in NJ this Fall.

Q: Our stories are so similar. I went through a lot of ups and downs, but I would not be here right now doing what I do if I had not have gone through those things. You know, the divorce and the homelessness and all the good decisions and the bad decisions. I always call it the journey, right? We go through our own journey. But I love that you call it a Quest for Better. Because isn't that really what's happening? We are trying to do the best we can. We are learning. Because of your experience, you're doing so well in your real estate with your team, because the people around you can see your heart and see how much you really care for them to reach better, because that's what we're all trying to do.

CG: That's right. You can't succeed without failure, and every single one of those failures breaks you open a little bit, expands you so that you can deal with the next one a little bit better and a little bit better every time.

I've learned you can't do it alone. Collaboration is key. My team was born out of the fact that I derive immense satisfaction from helping others grow and reach their potential. This collective of agents we are building in New Jersey is about relieving the struggle and supporting our agents so that they can go out and do what they do best to support the people and communities they serve. I believe an empowered agent is better able to empower their clients and that results in the best service possible.

Q: Of course. And, you know, I was just having this conversation last night. Failure is feedback. That's really it. Usually we think of failure as just the worst thing. It isn't. It is just feedback. Thank you so much for sharing that. We all have to go through something, we all have a story, so thank you for sharing yours. What is inspiring you now?

CG: On the business side. We have BIG things in store.

We are expanding our team and our services and we are going global! EXP has created so many opportunities and connected me with like minded people who are also on a mission to do BIG things. It is different here! We have a strong residential team and will continue to build and create a space for amazing agents and teams to join forces with us to build their business and serve their clients and communities.

We have added a commercial and global division to our services - Experience Global Inc. We have a great team in place with some serious talents and we can't wait to serve our clients in a holistic way. We will be providing a broader international platform and building pathways which help connect and serve our clients, the flow of information and investment opportunities.

We have also created a marketing agency – Experience Media Inc. We have always been avant garde with going the extra mile and creating the best marketing possible in our market to set our clients/ homes apart. We want to continue to offer this in a professional way to our clients and also now to our agent partners. We want our agents to not only use what we are putting out as our marketing but have marketing that speaks personally to them as well. Our marketing agency has customized packages for each of our agents where we create a logo, social media templates, seller and buyer packets, a buyer presentation, a listing presentation, business cards, sign panels, and mailers. It isn't just about me – the Experience NJ Team is a platform we want our agents to leverage to build their own presence. We fully recognize and support that in any way we can.

I now have a stellar team in place and can turn over the important day to day tasks and processes to those I've brought on who do them better than me! I can now focus on creating more opportunities, building out our divisions and continue to connect people and ideas, which is my passion.

As for what is inspiring me on a personal level? Healing and Getting in the flow so that I can continue to create the life I want and to be the mother I want to be to my son, Lucas.

I grew up in a household where parents were both hard-working immigrants. They are both self-made people and opened a business together and ran that successfully for over 40 years. My father was a very hard person to please. I also believe he still suffers from unhealed PTSD from war. Growing up with a father figure fighting his own battles affected me in some ways. Always seeking approval from him and never getting it - even to this day - can take a toll and erode your confidence. I know he loves me, but unfortunately what my father thought of me controlled my self-worth for far too long. Eventually, my husband's betrayal and ultimately my divorce didn't make my journey any easier.

But time has passed and I am moving past all of that, working on myself and learning to have healthier boundaries. I recently read a book called "Radical Acceptance" by the author Tara Brach. One of my favorite passages reads, "When we learn to trust ourselves and accept our imperfection, we cease to be at war with ourselves and others. We live with peace and grace." That's my personal mission for the coming year – to truly embrace this and continue to work towards more peace and grace. I'm starting to shed my armor. I'm coming to the realization that being vulnerable is a strength. All the things I went through have served as lessons and made me stronger, but I can now let them go and open space for the new.

Q: So good. I love that. What would you tell another woman who is maybe starting all over, maybe she had a downturn in her life. What would you tell her to do first to get it going again?

CG: Get a coach and seek out mentors. Success leaves clues and who you surround yourself with matters. Also, accountability is key. Get in the right rooms! Go to conferences, take courses, expand your mind!

Question the traditional models versus the new models. Changing my environment has changed my world. Change is hard and very few agents look to change companies with all the pain involved. They have been misled that all real estate brokerages are the same and that their business and life will be the same no matter where they are - but that could not be further from the truth.

Question what you know and make sure that you are building the foundation for your business and your life on healthy blocks and truths, instead of assumptions and beliefs that may not be true or useful. Everybody has to take that journey on their own and do some introspection about what their beliefs are. It's in there, whether you think it is or not. So take the time and space to excavate and realize what's true and what will serve you well. Align yourself with people who inspire you, support you and urge you to look within yourself for the answers. How do YOU feel about it? What do YOU think you should do to meet a particular challenge? It's not always the easy route, but it is the best and the surest way to find peace and clarity to move forward. I'm still on the journey. I don't think the journey ever ends, but I'm seeing glimpses that I am on the right path and it feels right to me.

Q: Oh, my goodness, Caroline, this has been an amazing conversation. Thank you so much for your vulnerability. I love when I talk to boss ladies and they can just tell you how it is. I know that people listening to this are going to be so inspired. How can people find you if they want to ask you a question, find out a little bit more about your team, find out more about real estate?

CG: Our website is ExperienceNJteam.com, for The Experience New Jersey Team. We offer:

- Access to the best tools, training, coaching and technology.
- Access to the top Titans of the industry to help them grow.
- Access to the opportunity to build equity in the fastest growing real estate company on the planet.

We are building an amazing collective of agents in NJ and across the globe and I am happy to talk shop with anyone who wants to hear more and be a part of it!

You can find our team on Facebook "The Experience NJ Team" and my personal page is under "Caroline Gosselin". Same thing on Instagram: @CarolineGosselinNJ for my personal page and @theExperienceNewJerseyTeam for our business page.

Q: Awesome. Thank you so much. I look forward to talking to you soon.

CG: Thank you, Tam. Always a pleasure to talk with you!

CAROLINE GOSSELIN

Caroline Gosselin is the Founder and CEO of The Experience NJ Team at EXP

Realty. Guided by her passion and dedication for superior service, expertise in media and marketing, and love for people, Caroline has constructed one of the fastest-growing real estate teams in the area. With guidance and leadership, she and her team have closed over $300 million in sales, establishing their expertise in the Northern New Jersey Market.

Always an active volunteer and impassioned supporter of women entrepreneurs, Caroline co-founded the local chapter of the national women's business group called "Believe. Inspire. Grow." (BIG). To commemorate her achievement, in 2011 she received the "Mover and Shaker" award from her local Chamber. In addition, she also served her community in her role as officer in her local Rotary Club for 4 years, and in 2015, was given the honor of being selected as one of Top 25 New Jersey Leading Women Entrepreneurs in NJ Monthly Magazine and in 2020 was dubbed a "Force for Change" by NJBiz.com.

As a talented marketer, Caroline has remained on the cutting-edge of the latest digital strategies to garner maximum exposure for the properties she represents. Effectively utilizing her affiliation with EXP Realty, she successfully leverages media opportunities with Zillow, the New York Times, the Wall Street Journal, and many others.

Her educational background set the stage for her success in real estate. She received her BA from the University of Texas at Austin, and her MA in International Relations in Paris, France. While Caroline has over 15 years of experience in the real estate industry, she began her professional career in the travel industry and then as a Program Manager for a NYC-based non-profit affiliated with the United Nations. She remains a top producer in the competitive world of real estate by utilizing her fluency in French and conversational Spanish.

Caroline is hosting the largest brand-agnostic real estate conference in the Tri-State area, bringing together world renown coaches and speakers for a one-day exclusive event, known as "The Quest Conference". A firm believer that a better life leads to a better business, she decided to create an amazing opportunity for those in the industry to collaborate, network, and invigorate their business.

Leave time and space for you to think through what you're about to do and what your feelings are and what your gut says.

—*Caroline Gosselin*

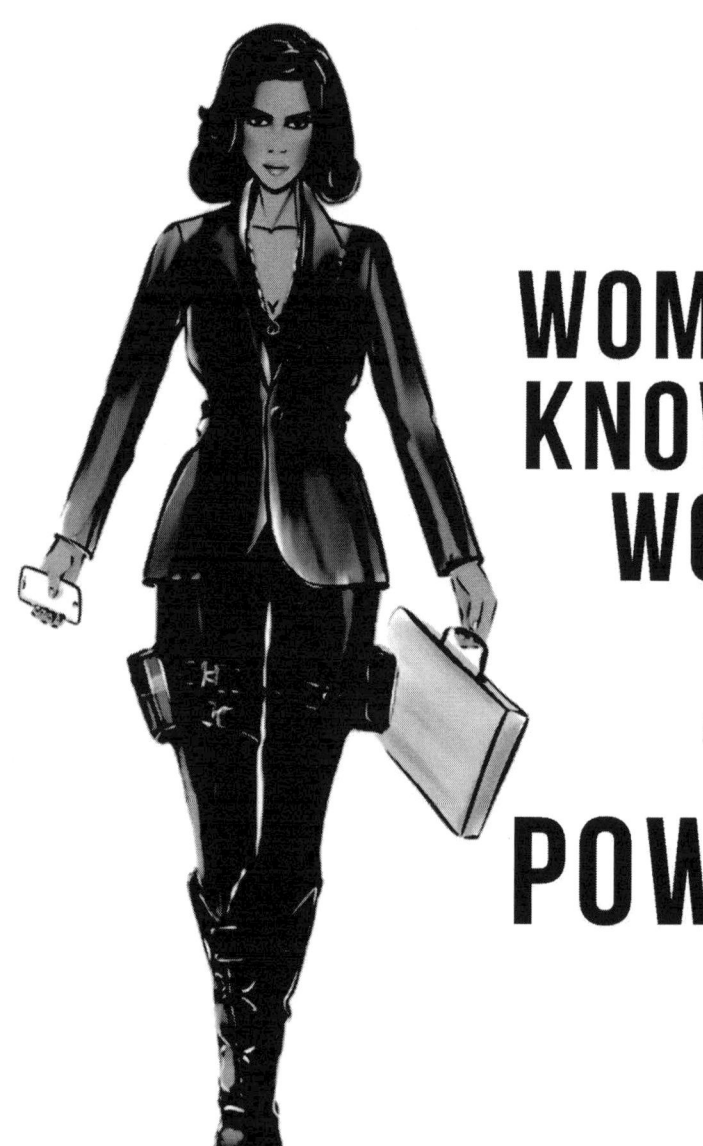

WOMEN WHO KNOW THEIR WORTH

ARE

POWERFUL

SECTION 2

Business

TARA MCCARTHY
House Addicts EXP Realty
Owner/ Realtor

CHAPTER 7

Continue to Think Bigger, Be Bigger, Be More Influential and Be More Helpful

with Tara McCarthy

HEY THERE, SUPERWOMEN. I AM SO EXCITED TO have my next guest. We've been talking to some amazing women who are creating some incredible companies and today we've got one who is not only a realtor developing a big team, but she also has this concept that I find incredible—the Girls With Grit Collective. This is a way that she's thinking about business, a way she is helping women in real estate to go a little bigger, a little broader, and I really want to share this with you. So let's get to it. The name of her real estate company is House Addicts, she's brokered by eXp Realty, and then she also has the Girls With Grit Collective. So let's talk to her about all of it, about what is possible, about where you can go within real estate when you start thinking outside of the box.

Q: Tara McCarthy, how are you?
Tara McCarthy: Hello. I'm awesome. Thank you so much, Tam. It's so great to be here.

Q: Yes. I am really excited to have this conversation. Before we start jumping into the nitty-gritty of it, everybody gets into real estate in a little different way. Tell me the way you got into real estate and what inspired you to do it?
TM: I joke that I was born into real estate. My mom was a new-home salesperson. She sold new construction. My dad was a general contractor, and so real estate was just kind of part of our family. My very first job, when I was trying to save money to buy a car, was working for the company that cleaned the houses for my mom's new-construction community. My first big job was as the weekend receptionist at a Keller Williams office in my hometown. So honestly, real estate has always been part of my life. I know a lot of people may see a TV show or go through the home-buying experience and think, "Oh, I'd love to do that, this would be such a great job."

But for me, it was just my calling. And, you know, the cool thing about real estate is that obviously you're helping people buy and sell homes. But more importantly, I feel like you're really able to be a shepherd of their journey, right?

You're helping them build monumental wealth in their lives. So I think that's what's kept me in real estate, if that makes sense.

Q: Yes, it's really true. Real estate is a shelter, but it's so much more than that. It is the biggest purchase you'll probably make, it is determining the place where your kids are going to go to school. Some of the biggest decisions in your life are related to the real estate choice you make. And it is one of the smartest things you can do because it is one of the only ways that some people are able to build any sort of wealth in their life. If you have property, you can start building equity and leveraging that. How did your real estate career evolve?

TM: This is my 17th year in the business and I really worked my way up through the ranks. I mentioned that I was a receptionist at a real estate office, and then I moved into an administrative position with a builder. Then I went into sales for the builder. I sold new construction for many, many years before I decided to move into the resale market. That's kind of a funny story. I had just started dating my now husband and we'd just had, like, the third snowstorm in as many weeks in Colorado. And I was done. I don't like cold weather, I don't like snow, so I was thinking, "Where should I move?" And this was in 2009 when the market was terrible, right? So I did an online survey of where I should move based on my interests and the first result was San Diego. Well, I knew I couldn't start over in San Diego. We were in a down market, I didn't have the money to do that. But the second choice was Scottsdale, so I started doing some research on Scottsdale. And within five weeks, my now husband and I had picked up and we moved to Scottsdale.

It was probably one of the scariest days of my life. I walked away from a salary and a lot of commissions, but I was just like, "You know what? This is not what I see for myself for the rest of my life, and I'm going to start something new." And there was something really powerful behind that, being able to just, like, burn the boats, right? There is no backup plan; you just go. And my husband and I thought we would be down there for a year, flipping houses. We ended up staying for almost five years and flipping a little over 200 houses.

By the time we left, we had built a business that was in the multiple millions of dollars and we had about $200 million in buying power. We had a big operation. So that's really where I learned about how real estate can be leveraged for wealth. Because up until that point in time, I didn't know anything about that. I thought you just bought a house to live in. So during that time, I learned, honestly, how real money is made, right? Like, real money. Not employment money, not salary money, but generational wealth type of money. And as the market improved in Scottsdale, it wasn't so good for us as investors, but at the end of our time there, as we came back to Colorado, we had really learned what kind of team we wanted to build here and what we wanted to build a team around.

Like you just said, it's so much more than real estate. One of the biggest disconnects in our industry, I believe, is that nobody talks to each other. Your financial planner isn't generally talking to your real estate agent, and your financial planner isn't generally talking to your mortgage broker. So there's a lot of disconnect about how your money is being used and where your investments are. Because for most people, their home is their largest financial asset. A lot of my clients made more money on their homes in the last three years than they did at their actual jobs that they went to 40 hours a week. So what we try to do, our value proposition, is that we build the bridge between all three of those areas.

And so rather than just representing somebody—like, you call me and tell me you want a four-bedroom house in this city and this is your budget—we really look at it as an overall picture. We say, "Okay, so how does this play into your actual long-term wealth goals?" Because for a lot of people, they'll say, "Oh, well that house is only $200 more a month. We can afford that; we'll not eat out one night a week." And a lot of agents will say, "Yeah, do that. Don't eat out. Buy the bigger house." And for us, I'd say, "Yeah, but that $200 a month, if we place that with your financial planner and you put it in an account that is going to grow exponentially with compound interest, that's going to be $1 million dollars in 20 years." So, like, do you really care about this house? Or can we hang with this other house, right? So that's the kind of real estate team that we built and how we built our business. We are a true fiduciary to our clients in all ways, not just their real estate piece, if that makes sense.

Q: That is so incredible. Because a lot of people don't go into real estate thinking about their financial goals. They're not always thinking about what this is going to look like on my balance sheet. They're not looking at all those pieces. Usually, that's an investor. An investor and a homeowner are not necessarily the same person. But you're really marrying the two and saying, "You know what? This is an investment, so you have to think about this as an investment and part of the overall picture."
TM: Absolutely. It's about the entire portfolio, right? A lot

of our clients now have built six figures worth of equity in their homes in a very short period of time. And so it's like, okay, you're earning 3.5 percent or 4 percent on your money because that's what you're saving in your interest rate. But if we reinvested that in another way, maybe it's with an investment property or maybe you're doing a short-term rental or maybe you invest in a more traditional avenue. Then how can we continue to grow your wealth over the course of all parts of your life?

Q: I love that. So I know it hasn't always been easy. Your group is called Girls With Grit, and when you say grit, that alludes to having to get through some difficulties and still keep going, you know? Being able to have a little bit more fortitude, a little bit more backbone, you know, some big ovaries and really pull off some things.

TM: For sure. So for me, I moved out of my house when I was 16 years old. I had not graduated high school at that point. I never graduated college. I was on my own a lot when I was really young, right? Looking back, I was maybe kind of stubborn. It wasn't a running-away-from-home situation. That wasn't it. I was just like, "Nope. I'm on to the next chapter of my life now." So there's a certain amount of grit that comes with that, right? When you're going to school and you're working and you're your own provider. There is no plan B. You have to make it work.

And I think that's a common thread I find in some of the most influential people in my life. They are people who really had an uphill climb at some point in their life. For some it was when they were young; for others it's when they were older. And I mean, I made a lot of bad decisions when I was younger that I had to overcome. I always say that you are living your life today either because of your choices or in spite of your choices. Maybe you're living a good life today because you made good choices or you might be living a good life today in spite of the bad choices that you made, right? I also think that my experience is what built a lot of belief in myself, a lot of independence. You just figure it out. To a certain extent, you don't rely on anybody else.

Q: That's very inspiring, because that shows that it's possible, right? You made it, you were able to create great success, and not by doing it in a prescribed way where people said you have to go this way and there's no other way to do it. In spite of the difficulties that you had, you figured out your way. That speaks to a lot of people out here who have had to make some difficult choices or they were stubborn or whatever the situation was, and they can look at you and say, "Hey, if Tara can do it, I can do it." And I think real estate is a great vehicle for that, because it allows you to create great success, great wealth.

TM: If it wasn't for real estate, I would be living a completely different life. There are not a lot of industries where you can come in and make multiple six figures, seven figures of income, without a college degree. Real estate is one of those areas where you truly can be anything that you want to be. On the flip side of that, though, real estate is an incredibly difficult business to be successful in. You have to have a lot of grit in order to be successful. I mean, the failure rate is over 90 percent in the first five years now.

Actually Girls With Grit was born out of that. We have to do better for ourselves. And so Girls With Grit is a female-based group that started out as just like a collaborative environment where we could come together and we could be a support for one another. I say collaboration is the new currency, right? Or as some people say, your network is your net worth. Who is around you? Who is going to help pull you up the ladder when you feel like you can't do it yourself? And Girls With Grit is not just my baby: I partnered with two other really incredible women, Jamie Tulac and Lauren Rocco, on building this place where women like us, who'd had a tough time, who didn't have somebody to really mentor us or show us the right way to success, where we could be that guide or that Sherpa for women in the real estate industry. It's funny, because I feel like real estate tends to attract women who have persevered through some sort of bad situation. Whether it was a home life situation or a divorce or maybe they're a single mom or whatever it is, and they just need somebody to show them it can be done. And that's what we're trying to do.

Q: And you're doing it and that's incredible. What's inspiring you right now? What is really driving a lot of this? Girls with Grit is an incredible idea, but it's not easy to do that alongside your thriving real estate business and maintaining your team. So tell me, what is inspiring you to do all that?

TM: I've always been very, very competitive in my life. I thrive on competition, I like to be number one. I'm the type of person who will do what it takes to win. Not at all costs, but at the same time, I will win, right? I'll figure it out. But the first time that somebody won because of something I taught them, it was 100 times more fulfilling than me winning myself.

And so I had not had that experience before. I was a trainer when I was in new-home sales, but it wasn't the same. And so when that stuff started happening inside of our group, it just fueled us so much more to continue to grow and to think bigger and think about how many more people we could reach. So our mission in Girls With Grit is to touch one 100,000 women in real estate and influence their business in a positive way.

Whether that's teaching them how to be a single agent, whether that's teaching them how to leverage so that they can have a better home life, whether that's teaching them how to build a team, it's not about what we teach them, it's about how we help them reach their own goals.

And, honestly, that's been a little bit of an obstacle for me too, right? Because one thing that I've learned is we've built this thing, it's growing so fast, as of today we have 8,500 people in our group. But it's a tremendous responsibility for your vision to be big enough for everybody else's vision to fit inside of it. I never want to feel like somebody comes into our group and is like, well, they're not thinking big enough for me and now I have to find something else. And so it's like, how do we continue to think bigger, be bigger, be more influential, be more helpful. So that's part of my passion for it too. I like challenges. And so, we get to help people, which is super fulfilling. I can't tell you how much I love the text messages I get when they're like this strategy that you taught me, I just got my first listing, I just got my first million-dollar listing, I bought a car with the money—it's insanely fulfilling. It's so cool.

Q: It's so cool. I love what you're doing. How can someone find you? I know there are women who want to 10x or just boss up or do whatever in real estate, and they're going to want to connect with you.

TM: My personal handle on Instagram is @thisistaramccarthy. Girls With Grit Collective is the name of our Facebook group—look for the Facebook group, not the page. And then you can always grab my contact information on my website too, which is www.houseaddicts.com.

And if I could just leave everyone with one little small thing, it's that I would encourage anybody who feels even slightly inspired by this to just do the thing. Whatever it is, just do the thing and feel confident that not doing the thing is always going to be a failure, but you have the opportunity to grow in so many ways if you just do what you're being called to do.

Q: Do the thing! Tara, thank you so much. I'm excited for everything we're going to be doing this year.

TM: Thank you, Tam. Thank you for having me.

TARA MCCARTHY
www.houseaddicts.com

Tara McCarthy "grew up" in real estate you could say. Tara started her real estate career as her Mother's (who sold new construction) unpaid assistant and her first 'big kid' job as a receptionist for Keller Williams. She's never left!

Tara spent 10 years selling new construction for national home builders prior to taking on a role as the VP of Sales & Marketing for a private builder in Denver. In 2009 she, and her now Husband Cody, relocated to Scottsdale Arizona knowing not a single soul.

Within 3 years Tara was managing a multi-million dollar flipping enterprise with 20+ employees & purchasing power in excess of $250 million dollars. She & Cody flipped over 200 homes prior to moving back to her home state of CO in 2014.

Tara has since built a successful real estate business with partners across the nation & sells over $30m in personal production, while continuing to flip homes. Her passion now lies in working with other agents to build the businesses of their dreams.

When she's not running her business, you'll find her traveling and spending time with her Husband and two sons, Quinton (13) and Caden(6).

The first time
that somebody
won because of
something I taught
them was one
hundred times more
fulfilling than me
winning myself.

— *Tara McCarthy*

In order to lead others, you have to really be able to lead yourself.

—*Nikki Klein*

NIKKI KLEIN
Brilliant Living, Founder and Realtor

CHAPTER 8

Communicate What You Do
with Nikki Klein

HEY THERE, SUPERWOMEN. I AM SO EXCITED today to have my next guest. I just told this amazing woman she's now my new favorite person. Because she's doing such an amazing job. Not only is she in real estate, which you guys know I love, but she also has an understanding of marketing and getting herself out there that I'm excited for her to share. She's been in real estate for about seven years and she's created an amazing team down in Boca Raton, Florida.

Q: Nikki Klein, how are you?
Nikki Klein: I'm doing well. Thank you.

Q: Awesome. First of all, what inspired you to go into real estate and how did you end up in Boca?

NK: I always had an interest in real estate. And I guess I had this feeling that one day I would be in real estate. I moved to Florida, I didn't know anybody, and we didn't have the best experience when we were buying our house. And I thought to myself, well, if this is the standard of real estate here, I'm going to just get my license and sell a few homes. And I ended up getting my license and selling a lot of homes! And it just became my passion.

Q: Did you join a brokerage? When did you decide to start a team?

NK: I was at one of the biggest brokerages out there. I hung my license with them until about six months ago, actually. It was amazing. They basically grew me into the agent that I am today. I was an individual agent for many years. Then I wanted to grow a team and I just kept "failing forward" at it. I kept trying to build a team and it would implode and I really feel like it was because I just wasn't ready. I wasn't ready to build the team that I have today. So I went through a lot of trial and error, a lot of failures. Lots of wins, too, but as far as building the team, that was my biggest struggle.

Q: Probably a lot of people would say so. Building a team, you have to learn a couple of new things. I mean, you can motivate yourself, but now trying to duplicate yourself is a whole different thing, I would imagine. What are some obstacles you had to work through, whether in life or in business?

NK: I got divorced a few years ago, so that was a bit of a struggle. Because that is a very emotional process—it's like a death, really. You have to go through the death of the life that you had or that you thought you were going to have. I have three kids, so I'm parenting my kids and also running a business. So it was not easy. Oh, and I also got diagnosed with ADHD.

Q: Oh, wow. Well, you know what? I think about ADHD and I know it's a struggle. But I think it's a benefit, too.
NK: Oh, I love it. I mean, it is my superpower. I can do multiple things. And you know what? It's funny, because my strategic business partner said to me, you have such a short memory, but such a quick mind.

Q: Yes.
NK: It's so true. I have a very short memory and a very quick mind. So I could handle all these different tasks, but then I'm like, what was that thing I just told you 10 minutes ago? It's definitely my superpower, though. It has helped push me forward, and it wasn't easy. Being a single parent and running a business and a household and on and on, having ADHD and trying to figure out how to make food for children that eat all the time, it's a struggle.

Meanwhile I also have done a lot of work on my self-development. I think that in order to lead others, you have to really be able to lead yourself. And I've done a lot of work on myself. I've read a lot of books, I've done a lot of coaching, I've been to retreats. You name it, and I have done it. And then I felt like I was ready. I was ready to make a move to another brokerage. I was ready to start building a team. And it all aligned when it was supposed to.

Q: So good. I'm glad you brought up just doing the work because we all still have things, traumas that we have dealt with in our young lives, or going through divorce— like you say, there are things you have to work through. And people need to know that is okay! You'll still make it. You'll still be successful in business.

NK: One hundred percent. I think that it makes you look back on the things that you've done in your past and heal the trauma from that. And you just think in a different way. I just finished reading Michael Singer's book, *The Surrender Experiment.*

Q: I love those books. I love them.

NK: It was amazing. And it validated how I feel about just allowing the universe to kind of guide you. And whenever you have a thought in your mind, or a judgment, or you think, "I don't want to do this" or you are presented with something, just go with it, and see what happens. Go with the flow. It's amazing.

Q: I agree. I learned so much from *The Surrender Experiment*. I love that. Those books are so good. So what is inspiring you right now?

NK: I really like to do things. My team likes to say, "We follow the fun." So what is inspiring me right now is the fact that I'm opening a new office and that I'm able to connect people in a way that I don't know if many people have been able to connect their community. Watching my agents grow, watching them self-discover, I'm just inspired by the ripple effect. When I see things happening around me that help the world in general, or even an individual, those are the sorts of things that inspire me.

Q: I love that. Do you work with people all over the U.S.?

NK: So we sell houses in Florida, but we help agents across the world.

Q: That's very cool. What would you tell another real estate agent who is looking to be successful but is new in this business?

NK: It's really about communicating what you do. I think a lot of people are silent agents, right? They're not out there saying, "I sell real estate." When I first started, I would be in the grocery line and I'd be like, "Oh, I'm just so exhausted." And people would be like, "Well, what do you do?" And it instantly opens up the conversation. "Oh, I sell real estate." Then they'll say, "Well, how's the market?" I'll say, "It depends. Are you looking to buy, sell or invest?" So it just is having those conversations, making it very clear. I mean, even if you have to wear a name tag with your brokerage on it! Just being out there and letting people know what you do is key. Don't be shy, don't be a secret agent.

Q: I love that. Give me some of the ways that you would suggest agents be more visible out there, social media tips or events or other ways to avoid being a secret agent.

NK: One of the things agents do that I always advise *against* doing is posting every sale or listing without context or a story. People need a story. They want their heartstrings tugged, they need some emotion behind what's happening. If your dental hygienist tells you, "I just cleaned more teeth." "I just cleaned more teeth," that's not very interesting. But if she told you a story, like, "This person just came in and they had bit into an apple and broke a tooth and there were chunks of teeth everywhere and I had to go through it," it's a much more compelling story.

So don't write a social media post that says "I just showed a house" or "I just sold a house." For example, when I was a new agent, what I would do in order to get more traffic is take strategic photos. Let's say I was showing some condos that were, like, $1,000 a month to rent, and that was my client. But across the river, there were $5 million homes. What I would do is take a photo across the river and say, "I am really enjoying my showings today." It would give the perception that I was showing these $5 million homes, when in fact I was showing the condos behind me. And I used to get messages from people, like, "You're doing so well, can you help my sister who's moving here?" Perception is everything in this business and in marketing as well. It's how you phrase things and how the audience is going to perceive it.

Q: Absolutely. I love this. How can someone find you, Nikki, if they are interested in becoming an agent, interested to know a little more about real estate or the Boca Raton market?
NK: You can reach me at nikki@thebrilliantteam.com or text me at 561-325-9687. You can also find me, Nikki Klein, on Facebook. I'm always active on Facebook and I would love to connect. Whatever questions you have, however I can help you, I'm here and available.

Q: Thank you so much. I look forward to everything we're doing together.
NK: Thank you, me too.

NIKKI KLEIN

www.thebrilliantteam.com

Nikki Klein is nationally recognized as one of South Florida's foremost real estate experts. Since she joined the real estate industry in 2014, Nikki has closed more than $250,000,000 in transactions as an independent agent and worked with hundreds of clients.

Nikki achieved this success through a steadfast commitment to her vision of positively impacting people's lives and the community through real estate. Nikki is a focused listener, an able advisor and a fierce, yet fair, advocate. Known for her intuition and diligence, she creates a positive experience for both sides in any property transaction. Her business approach is direct yet compassionate: she listens to the client's needs, matches them to the right property and ensures an honest and efficient transaction.

Driven by her passion to build and serve the community, Nikki founded Boca Raton Mom's Connect, the largest growing Facebook group in the Boca area with over 22,000 members. The group connects parents and caregivers in the greater Boca area for support and resources and hosts numerous family, community and charity events each year.

Nikki is a native of London, England who fell in love with South Florida during her time as a University of Miami undergraduate. She spent the better part of two decades in New York and Connecticut before choosing to return to Florida. Prior to her real estate career, she enjoyed a diverse career including planning large-scale events for several major organizations and being an on-air personality for MTV London.

JAMIE TULAK
Jamie Sells Raleigh
Real Estate Broker and Designer

CHAPTER 9

Stay in Your Lane, Put your Head Down and Focus on You

with Jamie Tulak

HEY THERE, SUPERWOMEN. I AM SO EXCITED TO have my next guest. I've been talking to some amazing women in real estate. You guys know how much I love real estate, because I was in real estate for a long time. This young lady that I'm talking with today has an amazing real estate business as well as a side business—or a runaway train, they might say at this point! It's amazing. I'm so proud of these women, so amazed by what they've created in such a short time. One of the things that I have learned over the years is that success always leaves clues. So that's one reason I love doing podcasts. I have learned so much, even about my own business, every time I have done an interview.

Q: Jamie Tulak, how are you doing?
Jamie Tulak: Good! Thanks, Tam, for that introduction. You make us sound awesome.

Q: You are awesome. So let's get listeners caught up on what we're talking about. First of all, you're from North Carolina?
JT: I'm from California originally, but now I'm in Raleigh, North Carolina. I've only lived here for the last three years. I was born and raised in California. I could share my story with you. How much time do we have?

Q: Yeah! Tell me your whole story. How did you get to North Carolina?
JT: Let's back this fast-moving train up a little bit. I was raised in a little farm town called Hanford, which is about 45 minutes south of Fresno, California. I went to Fresno State and got my degree in interior design. The market was crashing back then, and I went into real estate on a whim. It was actually by accident that I tumbled into real estate because I went to go get a job in the design field and ended up connecting with a custom homebuilder thinking I was getting a job in design, but it was actually a sales job.

I loved it so much that I ended up leaving that builder, took a leap of faith, and told my husband, 'I'm leaving this little job that I was getting paid peanuts for, I'm going to go get my real estate license, in a crashing market, and we're going to do something with this." I said to him, "Without a shadow of a doubt, I hear God calling me to this and you cannot tell me to disobey. I'm going to follow this and we're going to make a life out of this." I thought he was going to divorce me right then and there. But he supported me, I love him, we've been married now for 11 years, so he's been alongside me for this entire journey.

In my first year I ended up selling nearly 35 houses in a down market and I knew I was where I was meant to be. Then one thing led to another, I got him out of the corporate world, and we ended up starting a real estate team together. We also started a home-staging company and opened up a retail design storefront, selling some of the styles we would stage with. We had our little mini empire. We were in Lemoore, California, and people called us the Chip and Joanna Gaines of that small town. We were building our little mini empire together.

The whole staging theme came about on a whim also. I had an awesome client, a dear family friend of ours, who had a condo that was right across the street from a cemetery on a very busy road. Let me tell you, in that area, condos aren't a big deal. In fact, you don't buy a condo there. You mostly buy single-family residences. So I already had my back up against the wall. Then you have a really busy street and then you have a cemetery right across the road, which some people have very hard feelings for one way or the other.

It wasn't selling and she came to me two months later and said, "This is the longest that we've not had a tenant. We really need to figure this out." I prayed over it, and I came back to her the next day. I said, "I talked to my husband, and we came up with this idea. Do you think it would be OK if we staged your condo? Maybe we can figure it out. We'll remarket it, take new photos, and do all of that." Again, this was seven years ago in a small town. No one knew what staging was.

Maybe they saw it on HGTV. She said, "Sure, let's try it out. I trust you." It took us two weeks, because I had to go buy new furniture and everything, and I didn't know what I was doing. It was my first time. But we staged it, re-photographed it, remarketed it, and the very next day we got her a tenant.

I didn't make any money on that. In fact, we lost money on that deal. But she was very grateful, and they sent us a ton of amazing gift cards. I didn't make a commission, but I knew I was doing the right thing. At that moment we realized we were onto something. So that's how we built out our entire huge brand. In the midst of that, we had two kids. So I had a toddler at my knees and a baby on my hip, and something had to give. Something had to give because here I am with three small businesses and these two children. I knew that's not what God had for us. That life that we were living was chaotic. It was stressful. I didn't want to just let life pass us by and not enjoy any time with our kids. I knew that there was a better life, and I just didn't know what that looked like.

So we prayed over it and shut down our shop. Getting back to the question that you originally asked me, how did I end up in North Carolina, we prayed over it that week. My husband, who's originally from Pittsburgh, went to college in North Carolina for a couple of years. After 9/11 he joined the Navy, and the Navy took him out to California. That's how we met. So he had roots in the Raleigh area and we had visited here years ago, and I told him if we got married and had a family, I would love to raise a family in Raleigh. It's a beautiful place. It's a great area.

There are a lot of opportunities and so many colleges and universities within a five- or six-hour drive. So we finally did it. We shut down our shop and knew that was our next step. I said, "We're not trees. We're not stuck. We can pick up a move." Right? There's opportunity out there and we're going to take it. This was in June 2018 that we decided to do that—quietly, because you know how it is in real estate. You tell people you're moving, and your business dries up overnight. We couldn't afford for that to happen to us. So we quietly planned our exit strategy and in June 2019 we sold off everything, relocated, and said, "Let's live our dream life."

We haven't looked back and it's been amazing, incredible, everything we thought it would be and more. We're truly happy here. That in the nutshell is how I got to Raleigh. It's crazy to look back and see God's hand weave throughout our entire story.

Q: What I hear is faith, trust, and vision. That's what I hear. Faith, trust, vision, and you listen. You listen to what you're being told, what God is putting on your heart, and you move. You don't second-guess, you don't mess around. You're just open and you're ready to move. I love that. It's worked out for you.
JT: Yep. I have a sign here in my office that I made in June 2018, a week before we decided to move. It says, "Always do what you're afraid to do." I've looked at that every single day when I started to get nervous and realized that we just had to step out in faith. It's really funny you said faith because I actually have that tattooed on my arm. That's how I live.

Q: Do you know what's funny? There's a little sign behind you that I didn't see before. It says, "Faith over fear." That's amazing, Jamie.
JT: That's really funny. You just pulled that right out and we've been talking for what—five, ten minutes? You already figured out how I live my life.

Q: So you got to Raleigh, North Carolina. You're doing your business with your husband, which I 100 percent respect because I work with my husband too. I love working with my husband. What are some ups and downs that you have experienced in your business or in your life?

JT: Do you know what the hardest thing is? I can speak to this. To any of the women that are listening to this, if you're a strong woman, it takes a really strong man to deal with a very strong woman. People ask me that all the time, and say, "You guys make it seem like it's all been roses," and it hasn't. We have our struggles in our personal life, our business life, and our marriage. Right? No marriage is perfect.

But what I'll leave you with when you ask me is that I would not have any of the success I have if it weren't for an incredibly supportive husband. He lets me just do my thing—and when I say "let," I don't mean I ask for permission. It's yin and yang. It's this relationship that whatever needs to get done at home gets done. I don't ever have to ask him to do anything. He sees the need and fulfills it, whether that's in our business or our home life with our children. It really does take an incredible partnership, and I think that is why in this generation we're seeing a rise of stronger women than ever before. Because men have finally recognized that they're not the only shining star. So it's been a challenge and it's been a struggle growing a business alongside him. But he recognizes my strong points and allows me to be who I am and doesn't quiet that. He doesn't dim my light at all.

Q: He's not threatened by that strength?

JT: He's not. He's like, "Don't mind. You're the breadwinner, that's fine. We're a team. We run everything together. We raise our family together, our business, everything." While there have been challenges, I think you have to take them in stride. You have to have a very strong partner that you can run alongside in this journey together. To those of you women, if you're single, I get it. I understand. You just have to have some type of support system for people that believe in your vision and are there to support you along whatever journey, your business that you're growing, whatever you're doing in your life. We need support. Human beings were not meant to go through life alone and if that's you, you need to find your tribe. You really do.

Q: It's so true.
JT: That's kind of how Girls with Grit, my other business, came together. I strongly believe that we need a tribe. Gone are the days of women feeling like we have to diminish each other. Just because you're congratulating another woman on her success does not diminish what you have done. We are stronger together and we need each other to empower one another. I think we really do need to continue lifting each other as we climb. We're all going to be better together for it.

Q: I agree. First of all, there's so much sky. There's plenty of sky for all of us to benefit. None of us are lacking any oxygen right now. There's plenty of oxygen for everyone. So if I win, it doesn't mean that you can't win. I think a lot of times it might be a mindset thing. But me helping you win is not going to take away from me winning.
JT: Exactly. It actually helps us win faster.

Q: One-hundred percent. What inspires you today? You seem to be someone who, like me, sees a need, gets in there, and gets into action. What is inspiring you right now?

JT: Well, the thing that's hard about real estate is it's a very demanding career. I've been doing this for almost 13 years now. After a while, it's like, "Gosh, what's next for my life?" I think there is always a next step. But the thing that's inspiring me right now is realizing that in my time in this career—and I started in this career really young—I have gained so much knowledge that I can share with others, that it helps me to empower them to reach their goals. It's very inspiring to me when I hear other women share their wins, and share that the things they're learning and being taught within Girls with Grit are helping them reach their goals. I can't even tell you how many times people come up to us or they send us messages that say, "Thank you for doing what you've been doing. You've changed my life."

I've never been someone who has people coming up and saying that and it's very humbling. I'm just going to tell you, it's very humbling to recognize that you've stepped into your power. I'm right where God needs me to be and, in turn, I'm able to impact others by just being who I am. It's not like I'm doing it for any sort of recognition or that I'm expecting this. To hear that you've changed people's lives is truly humbling.

It is inspiring to know the impact that is being made and that will continue to grow because the magnitude at which this fast-moving train is taking off at cannot be stopped. It's an entire movement for women in real estate that is a continual inspiration for me, even on the bad or hard days. Just like anything, yes, this is my job, it's my career and I'm passionate about it. We've had good days and bad days, but it's the inspiration that I get from all the women that are pouring back into that group we have that keeps me going.

Q: I love that. What advice do you have for women to be successful in whatever careers they choose?

JT: This is the hardest thing for us women to really wrap our brains around and actually do it, but my best piece of advice is to stay in your lane, put your head down, and focus on you. The more that you focus on you and stop worrying about what everyone else around you is doing and stop the comparison game, the more you'll realize that when you focus on what you have right in front of you and you put your head down, you're able to go further, faster.

I think that's hard for women because we're naturally, constantly comparing ourselves physically, emotionally, mentally—"Oh, so and so over there has more going on for her than I do. What am I doing wrong?" Sis, you're not doing anything wrong. Just focus on what you've got. It will multiply when you focus on what you've got in front of you, and you stay in your lane. I think it's so hard for us women to do that, though. It's easy to come out and say that, but to actually do it is another thing. Remember that what another woman thinks about you is none of your business.

Q: So true. It has nothing to do with you. Seriously.

JT: Seriously. This is another thing that I've learned recently. It was an aha moment for me: What you think someone else thinks about you is not reality. You're making that up in your own head.

Q: It's funny that you say that because I used to do this and I finally had a similar aha moment probably 15 years ago now. I started to say, "They aren't thinking about you." Right? I really did think people were thinking about me, like, "Girl, why are you doing that? Blah, blah, blah." But I finally got to the place where I realized, no, they're too busy thinking about their own stuff that they got going on. People are freaking busy. They're in traffic. They're dealing with their husband and the kids. They aren't really thinking about you. Nobody is. When that finally hit me, I was like, "OK, I have been wasting too much time worrying about what they are thinking about."

JT: It's true. That's my biggest piece of advice.

Q: I love that. You are doing some amazing things with Girls with Grit. You had a big event a few weeks ago. You have a fast-growing community. Explain to us what it is and how people can find it.

JT: Thank you for asking. Girls with Grit right now is my passion project. It inspires me to get up every day and continue to show up for these women. It started off as a very small idea. We wanted it to be a referral network for women in real estate. We didn't want it to be like a typical referral network where it's like those little pods where as soon as you see Raleigh, North Carolina, 100 people are, like, "Jamie Tulak," but yet they've never even worked with me and never sent a referral to me. We didn't want that. We wanted it to be a referral network where maybe we do some training in coaching and mentorship to help women really level-up and become a boss in their space and their market.

One thing led to another, and it literally has become an entire movement. So, one year later we're basically 10,000 women that we coach and mentor across the country. To put it simply, it is a community where women can collaborate and feel like it's a safe space to come together and learn. We do a lot of free training. We do some challenges and whatnot. We have a couple of live events every year. As you said, we just had our conference in St. Pete Beach, Florida. In-person and virtually we had over 500 women attend that event.

I would imagine our event next year will probably have 1,000 total, and it's just growing massively. The reason why is it's not about Jamie Tulak, it's not about Tara McCarthy or Lauren Rocco and my other business partners. It's about women collaborating and supporting one another, learning, and growing together. We've realized that when we lift each other as we climb, we can get a lot further, faster. So that's why it's grown. It's because women needed this space.

I can't even count how many women have come up to us to say, "Thank you for creating this movement and for creating this collaboration." This is only the beginning. It's been super crazy to see just one small idea, once you actually put forth the effort to build that idea, to see how it's massively grown in such a short amount of time. That's how I know we're right where we need to be. God has us here. He brought the three of us together and we're here to continue growing this. Our goal is to impact 100,000 women in real estate and bring them into the fold and help them level up their real estate careers.

We have our private Facebook group called Girls with Grit Collective. You can request to join that group. You can also find us on Instagram, and we have our website, girlswithgritcollective.com where you can find out more information about us.

Q: I love it. I wish you guys all the success in the world. If somebody's in North Carolina and they want to find out about your real estate business, how would they connect with you?
JT: Look me up on Instagram @jamiesellsraleigh or go to jamiesellsraleigh.com. I welcome all the referrals. I'd love to take care of your referrals.

Q: Thank you, Jamie. I look forward to all the stuff we're doing together.
JT: Thank you, Tam. I appreciate your time. Have an awesome day.

JAMIE TULAK
jamiesellsraleigh.com

After 10 years in the real estate industry Jamie and her family stepped out in faith and left behind everything they had in California to go after their dream of moving to North Carolina. According to Jamie, they had planned for the relocation for over a year, and it took a lot of prayers, faith, and hard work to execute their plan.

When they moved to North Carolina, Jamie knew she had to roll up her sleeves and get to work in order to build her business from the ground up, for the second time . She had no database, but she knew that her digital marketing skills would help her flourish again. She joined a brokerage that gave her the freedom to brand herself how she wanted to. Within a year, Jamie was again among the top 1% of solo real estate agents in her new market Because of this grit and hard work, it landed her on a show on HGTV which was such a natural fit for her since she has a background and degree from Fresno State in interior design.

Besides being a real estate agent, Jamie has a passion project called Girls with Grit, where they have created a safe space for women in real estate. They coach, mentor and train women from all different brokerages from all across the country. She co-founded this coaching collaborative with Tara McCarthy and Lauren Rocco.

When you focus on
what you have right
in front of you and
you put your head
down, you're able to
go further, faster.

—Jamie Tulak

LAUREN ROCO
The Rocco Group, Owner/ Broker

CHAPTER 10

Create a lasting impact beyond the traditional

with Lauren Roco

HEY THERE, SUPERWOMEN. I AM SO EXCITED TO be speaking to my next guest. She is not just a rockstar real estate agent, but she is part of a fast-growing community called "Girls with Grit Collective". We're going to hear about that as well as her journey into real estate and how she had to overcome certain mindset blocks in order to really step into her success.

Q: Lauren Rocco, how are you?
Lauren Roco: I'm good! Thanks for having me.

Q: It's great to have you. How long have you been in real estate?
LR: I've been in real estate for 19 years. It's gone by quick.

Q: What prompted you to start a business?
LR: I didn't want to punch a clock for somebody else. I was young. My mom was in real estate. Actually, both my parents were in real estate. And so, when I was 20, I was going to school for marketing and then just decided, "Why am I going to punch somebody else's clock? I'll just do my own thing." And so here we are.

Q: Wow. Was it because your mom was in real estate, and you saw that it could be a great career choice for you?
LR: Pretty much. I liked the flexibility. I got married young. I got married at 20 and started having kids at 23, so I just saw needing that flexibility for my family as it grew.

Q: Have you always done this business by yourself, or did you incorporate your husband or a team early on?
LR: My husband used to have his license and then we had the Great Recession in 2008, 2009, and since all four of us, my mom and dad and me and my husband were all in real estate, my dad and my husband decided to open a restaurant to support everybody because nobody was selling houses. So, my husband got out, but it was never really his passion.

Q: Tell me a little bit about that because I have a real estate license. I was doing real estate back then too. And it was a tough time for everybody. The whole economy was messed up. Tell me a little bit about how you got through that difficult time.
LR: I think I just didn't give myself an out, you know? I

decided, "You're just going to figure it out. You're gonna pivot". So, I started doing REOs and short sales along the Florida panhandle. I waited tables during the day, and I would go into the back room when it was slow and work leads from 2 p.m. to 5 p.m. when nobody was in the restaurant. So, I think I just had that attitude: I'm gonna do what I have to do and we'll get through it.

Q: Right. Do you think that helps you now? Real estate is cyclical.
LR: I think so. I can look back and see I've made it through. I've made it once. If it shifts, I'll make it through again.

Q: What do you think you learned specifically about shifts in the market?
LR: I learned that there's always opportunity. You just have to look in the right spot. And maybe it's not as big of an opportunity as at other times, but there's always opportunity. And then for me personally, it was like, "God is going to take care of me." It might not look like everybody else. But, you know, if I've got to wait tables and sell real estate for this season, then that's what I'll do. I'll wait tables and sell real estate and we'll make it through. So, I think it was just having faith, doing the hard things, and knowing I'd come out on the other side eventually.

Q: What do you think people really need to either have or find in themselves in order to make it through tough times like that?
LR: Grit. Is that one I can say?

Q: Totally. I was hoping you were gonna say grit. Actually, because you are also a co-founder of Girls with Grit, right?
LR: Yes, I am.

Q: Tell me a little bit about how that came about.
LR: Honestly, it didn't come about—it snowballed. That's what that did. Girls with Grit started out as something way different than what it is now. But it is definitely a testimony to what happens when you run with like-minded people, and you do it together. You learn that you can go a lot faster. There's no way that one of us could have single-handedly accomplished what the three of us have accomplished in the past year and a half. It was the power of true collaboration and running together with other people that are like-minded.

Q: It's impressive. Let's back up and describe what the Girls with Grit community is.
LR: Girls with Grit is a community that basically gives women permission to think big. I feel like it gives a woman permission to have a big vision and still feel like she wants to be present for her family. Because I think there's this gap in the industry. There are the part-time agents that don't sell a lot and then there are these big mega-teams that seem untouchable because they sell thousands of houses a year. And there wasn't really a space for women who wanted to be high-producing single agents, if that makes sense. And that's what we were. So, we thought, "We need to create our own community."

Q: So essentially you are teaching women how to be high-producing single agents.
LR: Yes, I would say that's definitely our niche. "Here's how you actually sell real estate." Because nobody teaches any of

that. They teach how to get your license or maybe how to do one specific thing, but they don't give you the nitty gritty in the middle, the piece that actually moves the needle. That's where a lot of us were struggling and so Girls with Grit is basically us teaching everybody else the things that we wish we'd been able to learn earlier.

Q: Very cool. What goals do you have for Girls with Grit?
LR: We want to impact 100,000 women. Right now, our group is at 9,300 members, so we've got a little bit of a way to go but that's the goal: 100,000.

Q: I love it. Will that help your own personal real estate business?
LR: I think it definitely gives us credibility. It gives us a platform amongst our peers, to be seen as leaders. But I don't know that it would necessarily translate into more deals from clients locally unless I leveraged it properly. But right now, that's not the goal.

Q: It's really a national thing more than anything.
LR: Right. I would say there's potential for agent-to-agent referrals. But the average person in Charlotte doesn't know anything about Girls with Grit, you know what I mean? They just want to know; are you going to list my house and do a good job?

Q: What advice would you give women who want to build a community like that? As you said, you go further, faster with a group, with a team.
LR: I think you have to really show up authentically. People have to buy into the community. They have to feel like you're

accessible. They have to feel like they're part of it. And they are, absolutely. They need to be able to take ownership of it. If it's all about one person and not about the community, they can't take hold of that. And I think that's been a huge asset for our growth, is just women feeling like they're a part of it. I feel like we've done a really good job letting them in. Letting them in when we don't do something perfect and we're like, "Hey, we want to do this better for you. Let's do this together."

Q: What is inspiring you right now?
LR: I think what's inspiring me right now is just impact. Being able to look back and be like, hey, this career that I built over 19 years, hasn't been for nothing. Because I could be out of the business. I could stop selling houses and then I would be done. Like my career is done. So, the fact that I'm able to impact people who are just getting started or maybe building a team or whatever, I feel like I'm able to have lasting impact beyond the traditional real estate sale.

Q: Nice. Is that your ultimate goal, to make a big impact?
LR: I think so. I mean, otherwise, what's the point? It's definitely not financial for me. Having a little extra money is nice, but I could go sell a lot of real estate and make money. Making money is not the issue. For me, it's definitely the impact.

Q: Is there anything else you would like to share with women in real estate?
LR: It's hard. I mean, it's hard. But don't give up. Your journey's not going to look like everybody else's and that's okay. Whether your goal is to do $5 million or your goal is to do $50 million, whatever your goals are, they're your goals and that's okay. So just give yourself grace. Every single day is a

new day, and we get to start over. If you wake up and have breath in your lungs, then God's given you another day so don't take that for granted. Look for the positive because Lord knows there's enough negativity in the world.

Q: That's right. There is a lot for all of us to deal with— especially those who are moms and businesswomen.
LR: I didn't mention this before, but my husband is in full-time ministry. So, I'm a pastor's wife and an entrepreneur, which is to say I don't fit in a box. So, for me, it's been embracing that I have certain gifts and I am using those gifts in a way that may not look traditional to people in the church, right? Because they might think I should just homeschool my kids and serve in the church.

I think all those things are awesome. For me, though, I know I'm making a bigger impact by serving my market-place, you know? And so just getting comfortable with how God has uniquely crafted each of us and using those gifts is important. If they're in the home, great. If they're out in the business world, that's great too. It took me a while to get comfortable saying that because I felt like I was doing some-thing wrong, which is horrible to say, but that's the truth.

Q: I know what that looks like. I was raised in a family of entrepreneurs and ministers as well. And I've always felt it was one of the things that held me back for a long time—maybe someone won't love me if I am successful. Like there's something wrong with that. So, I know exactly what you mean.
LR: Or that you're just out seeking material things because you're working really hard.

Q: That's right.

LR: That's been interesting to navigate, but I've matured through a lot of that. We're all still learning, but I feel like I've gotten on the other side of that. I'm comfortable with the gifts that God's given me. So, it's been cool.

Q: That's awesome. Where can people connect with you and find Girls with Grit?

LR: You can find me on Instagram @heylaurenrocco. My website is LaurenRocco.com. Or you can call me! My number is 704-990-9140. I'm just a text away. That's usually the easiest way to get me. The community website is GirlsWithGritCollective.com or @girlswithgritcollective on Instagram. Our Facebook group is for female agents so people can join us there, too.

Q: Lauren, thank you so much. I appreciate it.

LR: Thank you, Tam.

LAUREN ROCO

LaurenRocco.com

Lauren Rocco has been selling homes for close to 20 years. She started in the panhandle of Florida, not even old enough to buy a bottle of wine as a closing gift. Lauren has since built a multi six figure business as sits at the top 3% of all Realtors. She currently runs a large team nationwide and serves clients locally in Charlotte, NC. Lauren is a co-founder of Girls With Grit Collective, a community and coaching platform for female real estate agents.

She's a pastor's wife turned entrepreneur and refuses to fit into any box. Lauren has been married to Johnny Rocco for 18 years and has 2 boys,

Jude and Eli. She would take a taco over wine any day and would rather die than do a spreadsheet. Lauren is an Enneagram 7 to the core! She loves life and has a passion to help women find their purpose. Lauren lives by the quote "You are a child of God, playing small does not serve the world!"

Making money is
not the issue, for me
I think it's definitely
the impact, for sure.

—*Lauren Roco*

Take a big breath. Learn to recognize that you're experiencing an emotion and learn to manage that so that you can have the best outcome.

—Rosie Rodriguez

ROSIE RODRIGUEZ
Powerhouse Mortgage Inc
CEO, Broker, Banker

CHAPTER 11

Thinking Like a Man, Feeling Like a Woman

with Rosie Rodriguez

HEY THERE, SUPERWOMEN. I AM SO EXCITED today to have my next guest. I'm always excited to talk to another boss lady who is in an industry that I love, and as you guys know, I love real estate. Rosie Rodriguez is here, from The Powerhouse Group, to share the story of her 20 years in this business, how she built a team, going through different phases and challenges and ending up as one of the top earners in her company.

Q: Rosie Rodriguez, how are you?

Rosie Rodriguez: I'm really good. Thank you so much for having me here. It's very exciting.

Q: Real estate is not an easy industry. I think it's fun and a little sexy, but it's not always easy. What made you decide to go into real estate 20 years ago? And why did you go into business on your own?

RR: The story of my interest in real estate goes way back to being a little girl. My parents immigrated from Mexico, and they didn't really speak much English. We lived in a little studio apartment—six people in a studio apartment. I clearly remember the struggle that my father had in finding us a home. I remember when we transitioned—I was no more than eight years old and I saw him work, I saw the struggle, what he put together so that his family would have a home.

Unfortunately, what happened in the next few years was that my mother fell ill, and then my father fell ill. So there were a lot of struggles early on. My father was not able to work for about a year, then he ended up passing away from his illness. I was the first person to receive the phone call. The nurse shared with me that my father could no longer breathe, that he stopped breathing. I was 13. He was on a dialysis machine, and this is where everything happened. So that was my first experience with having to figure things out. We were still in that home and six months later, my mother's cancer came back. She'd had breast cancer years prior. Then 18 months later, she passed away from the cancer that had spread. Now I was 15, and I was the last person with my mom, in the hospital, before she passed away.

So, Tam, the thing, is I adopted an attitude of being really grateful at the time. I know I didn't have my parents very long, but I saw how much they loved us and how hard they worked to provide for us. They were always pushing "education, education, education," so over the course of the next few years, I was able to pick up and focus on how I was going to make them proud. How was I going to make something of myself? Because at the time, although we had a house, it was in the hood, quite frankly. We had gunshots at the corner, all kinds of stuff.

And unfortunately—to answer the very first question, going all the way back—when I was about 19 or 20 years old we ended up losing the house. I remember stopping at a phone booth down the street, calling someone I found in the phone book saying, "What can I do? How can I save this?" Then I realized that there wasn't anything that could be done.

It was then that I said, "We lost this house. One day I'm going to find a way to buy this house back because my dad gave everything to give that to us. So how am I going to do that?" I knew that I had to go to college, so was able to get myself into college. I ended up graduating from USC. My goal was to figure out how to do this thing called real estate and how to buy property so that my kids would never have to go through what we went through. That's pretty much how the whole real estate conversation entered my life.

Q: That is an incredible story. I know it happened a long time ago, but I'm sorry that happened to you so early on. It's amazing though when I see people who go through struggles like that, how they process it, and how you took what your parents did and decided how you were going to be. How many siblings do you have?
RR: There are three of us, my older sister, myself, and my

younger brother. This was another driving force, because my brother was nine years old when my father passed and 11 years old when my mother passed. I remember my father saying once, "I just want to be here long enough to see him get to 18 years old." Since that didn't happen, I took on a little mom hat. I was just really intentional about making sure that he made it through school and got into college.

I was married young. I got married when I was 21 years old, and I took my brother with me out of the hood because I saw kids starting to get into a little bit of trouble. He did graduate and he got his master's degree. Everything worked out. But when people ask me that question, they're like, "Wow, you were so young. How did that work out?" One is that I did have an amazing aunt who continued to be part of our life. She lived with us at the time and she took on that matriarch role. She worked, but she was there for us. So that's one big thing.

The second thing is that, I know this might sound silly, but I really didn't feel good about people, including my family members, saying, "Oh, poor you. You poor kids." I didn't feel poor, you know? I felt blessed. The circumstances were not ideal. However, I was so grateful for having them and for the example that they set in terms of hard work, family, and all those things. So I was determined to rise above that. I was determined to say, "No, don't feel sorry for me. There are people out there that have something they're going through, but I'm OK. I'm going to take what I have and I'm going to take it to the next level and figure it out."

You don't have a plan B when you're 15 and both your parents pass away. You just go and you just figure out how do I get to school? There's one thing: How do I get to school? What's this whole college thing? How does that work? How do we pay for food? I was working from the time I was 12 because my parents were struggling, and I knew that there wasn't any money coming into the household so I couldn't ask for things. I knew that I was a part of a family unit and in order for me to buy myself a new blouse or lunch money whatever it was I wanted, I had to make my own lunch money, right?

Q: Right. So how it happened early on set the stage. Here's Rosie as a young girl, now she's moving on, she goes to college, she gets into real estate. So, what happens then? Because it sounds like you just kept going, chasing, and pushing. Tell me what became of your career.

RR: In my very first job in real estate, I started on the lending side. When my husband and I got married, we actually bought our home. We closed on it the same week that we got married. I didn't understand anything, Tam. I just saw all this money that my husband and I had saved, and then my aunt ended up purchasing with us, and I saw all the money go there and I didn't understand this closing statement. I felt like there was a whole lot of money that went in and not a big difference in the mortgage, right?

Because I didn't understand that, I had decided that once I graduated—I was still in school when I was married—I would go back to the lender and see if he would hire me. I called him and said, "I'm going to call you when I'm done," and he said, "Okay, great." But when the time came, I kept calling him and he wouldn't call me back. He was a mortgage broker. So, I just opened up the paper and somebody was hiring for a loan agent or a loan account executive, whatever it was, and I interviewed. The funny thing is that my manager a few months later said, "You know, I'm going to tell you a story. When you came in you didn't really test high. I wasn't sure what you were going to do." But I was the top producer the first month and figured out how to do this whole business.

I did really well with that company. I was in the top 10 in the country, so I decided to open up my own mortgage operation. I did that at a high level, I was probably closing 15+ transactions a month through the whole mortgage operation. And out of a need for service, I ended up opening up an escrow corporation because we had so much volume that the service providers weren't able to keep up. Anyhow my journey led me to open up my very first real estate office in 2004.

And the reason I did that is kind of a fun story, especially for the women in the room. I saw this awesome opportunity to be a part of a company that at the time had all these systems and structures. I walked into a room, Tam, of about 15 people.

Let me first go way back to when I walked into USC. I thought the students there were a different kind of people. I thought these people were made different and their DNA is different because they got into USC. But when I started getting into group projects, I realized we're the same, we just came from different backgrounds. That was my first experience with, "Hey, level up, little girl. You can do this."

My second experience was walking into that room. I was in my 30s and everybody in there was easily in their 40s, 50s, even 60, maybe. They were icons in the industry, and I was walking in there, this little Latina with this little company, which was a good little company. But I was in awe because of all of these men in the room—and one other woman. I was like, "Man, if I can just run with these giants, what could I learn? How could I grow?" I wasn't necessarily looking at the dollars and cents behind the opportunity of owning an office. I was looking at the opportunity to grow and to learn from people that were doing things or had done things at a much higher level than I had. So that was my second opportunity where I got to tell myself, "Hey, you're leveling up, little girl. You've leveled up and you're here. What are you going to do with this now?" So that's how I ended up opening up a real estate office.

Q: That is so impressive and inspiring. I think a lot of times people hold themselves back just because they look around the room and make a decision instead of leveling up and realizing that they're people just like you and you can learn these things, too. You have grit and you can get in there and learn and grow. You've built an incredible business as a result. What would you tell a woman that she needs to do in order to be successful?

RR: That's a really good question. There are so many things that I feel I could pour into other women. I have the highest respect for other successful women for one reason. It's because I know that, in general, women have a much bigger load to carry. Along the way in that whole journey, I have three children. So, nursing in the break room and then coming out being the broker of the office. Sleepless nights, somebody gets sick, and the women are out at the dentist appointments or the doctors' appointments, and then they still have to come to the closing table, and get with the clients, and make sure that the chips are falling where they're supposed to and all those things.

When I see other women and I see how successful they've been in their space, their companies, and their area of expertise, the one quality that I tend to find in these women is that they have learned how to put their emotions aside, on the table, and put on the business hat. Because we do have an advantage and a disadvantage. The advantage with women is that we are able to function from our logical minds, right? Our business minds, our black and white, we understand numbers, we're creative and we can put things together and figure them out. That's awesome.

But we also have the nurturing side. We have the empathetic side, right? The person who can empathize with the other person and therefore come up with better solutions and resolutions to different situations. However, that is the part where it takes steps and layers of maturity to get to that level where you understand that just because you feel like things should be a certain way doesn't mean that is the right way.

It's being able to put those feelings aside and recognizing, "OK this is a trigger, this is something that isn't working," *and* "Great, now we put the business hat on and figure out how it's going to work." Being able to carry a conversation with the man across the room or the woman or whoever it is—the person across the room and being able to elevate that conversation based on the fact that you can think like a man, and you can feel like a woman.

That would be my best piece of advice. You're going to feel it, you can process it in your own time. But when you're in that big conversation or that big deal or the negotiation, whatever it is, put your business hat on. Take a big breath. Learn to recognize that you're experiencing an emotion and learn to manage that so that you can have the best outcome.

Q: I love that. Think like a man, feel like a woman. So good. What is inspiring you right now?
RR: I've been lucky enough to be in this business for almost

25 years. I've built four different companies that I oversee, plus rentals and investments and Airbnbs and all that stuff. You know, a little over 3,000 agents nationwide, I'm a national president of eXp Latino. It's an organization within our company.

What inspires me right now, Tam, is I've gotten to a point in my life where I have enough evidence of my successes. I have a track record. I know that if I put my mind to something it's going to happen and it's just a matter of a little bit of hard work and all that. What inspires me is really collaborating and elevating at a higher and higher level. I know now what I bring to the table. I'm confident that I bring life experience, business experience, investment experience, wealth strategies, all those things. I'm very excited about being able to sit at the larger tables, collaborating with bigger thinkers and coming together to not just co-create business or projects or all those things, but to have an impact.

What kind of an impact can we make? I'm not speaking about a local impact—even though those are important—I'm thinking about a global impact. Especially with the company that we're with. eXp Realty is a global company. The fact that we operate on a virtual platform allows us to pop into a room and talk to the broker of Mexico, of Spain, of Israel. So, if you knew, and we do, that everything is literally at your fingertips, even with the Zoom call or whatnot, then what *could* we do? What else is possible?

Q: I love that, just being able to think a little bigger. It's what I talk about when I say you have to have a vision for what is possible. What's inspiring you is the possibility of making a great impact on a lot of people. Rosie, how can women get in contact with you? I'm sure they're going to want to know all about Powerhouse Group. They're going to want to pick your brain about real estate. How do they connect with you?

RR: First, one of the things that I didn't share that I want to just throw in is two little passion projects that I'm working on. One is investing nationally and internationally and really creating lifestyle homes that we can share with other individuals and kind of apply the Airbnb model but from a luxury standpoint. So, I'm just kind of throwing that in, because that's super exciting, right? Imagine a house on the beach, butlers and sangria or something like that. That is what is possible at the click of a button.

The other thing is that I am starting a nonprofit organization that will support the basic needs of orphanages in Mexico. The next phase of that project will focus on higher education. But when I talk about "higher education," I'm not necessarily talking about math, I'm talking about the mindset and skills that will allow these children to graduate from the orphanage fluent in English, using technology, and things of that sort. The nonprofit should be done by the end of the year and I am calling it the Umboto Organization. The reason I share the name is because that was my mother's name, which translates to "shelter," interestingly enough.

I'm very excited about that. I've raised hundreds and thousands of dollars for different organizations, and this is the first time that I'm actually creating my own and I'm very excited about the impact I can make on hundreds of children in Baja California. That's my focus. The reason I picked that is because I can actually meet the kids. I can visit the kids and I can get involved. So that's one passion project. The other passion project, Tam, you're going to love this one. I created a corporation, and the corporation is called BAWS, Inc. It's pronounced like "boss," but BAWS stands for BadAss Women Succeeding.

Q: I love it. I'm getting goosebumps, Rosie.
RR: I'm inviting you to be part of our Board for sure.

Q: I would love to. We can definitely talk about that.
RR: Yeah. So, I planted the seed for that about five years ago and I haven't moved the needle on it yet, but I started doing a couple of interviews like this, just interviewing really successful, badass women. I would like to build an entire network in that space. So that's the other fun project. The difference between this group and some other groups out there is that I often see, Tam, that the topics sometimes tend to be around the nurture side, the feeling side, the challenges, and whatnot.

I think that's an important part of our story and it helps shape who we are. However, I'm much more interested in talking about your successes, your wins, your highlights, your goals, and your dreams. I'm excited about the badass in you that's going to take you and the people around you to the next level. I don't necessarily want to be in a therapy session. There's a space for that. I want to be in a room full of like, "Let's freaking go, girl." Like, "What the hell are we going to do?" and "Get out of the way because we're coming."

Q: I love that so much. That's exactly what we need right now, because we do have a lot of each other. We have plenty of each other and there's a place for it. But we also have to recognize that there are women that actually do want to succeed on a big scale. They are not playing around, they want success on a big scale. And I know that's possible.

RR: Yes. So those are things I'm excited about, obviously. You see my enthusiasm, right?

Q: I do, I do. You just completely lit up as you started talking about it.

RR: Yes! You see a lot of boardrooms full of men in suits, big money, and all the good stuff. Well, it's time for the ladies to have a boardroom, right? It's our business, baby. Let's go.

Q: That's right. Rosie, I'm so excited for you. Can people find you on social media typically or would they go to your website? What's the best way to connect?

RR: On Instagram I am @CallRosie. You can always send me a message there. I'm also on Facebook and LinkedIn. Reach me on IG for anything that has to do with real estate, business growth, wealth. I'm very passionate about building wealth and creating wealth and I'm always happy to help another lady go up.

Q: I'm excited about all the stuff we're going to be working on this year! Rosie, thank you so much for your time.

RR: Thanks, Tam. It's been great.

ROSIE RODRIGUEZ

www.powerhousemortgage.com

With over 20 years as a Real Estate Broker, and a Ton of painful ups and downs, Rosie has built 6 successful businesses and earning 7 figures in passive income from 9 different streams of real estate income.

She teaches agents how to avoid the painful mistakes, How to free up their time, and make the most amount of money in the shortest amount of time through proven systems, structure, and coaching.

- *Real Estate Multi-Business Owner*
- *Top 1% Inter-National Team Leader and Trainer*
- *Best Selling Author*
- *Strategic Business and Marketing Consultant*
- *Founder of "The PowerHouse Agent Network"*
- *I help Real Estate Agents Launch their own Teams and Branches all over the world.*
- *National real estate team with over 5000 agents Nationwide*
- *Airbnb portfolio - I can teach you*
- *Real Estate Investment Advisor and Strategist - Let's do the numbers !*
- *Business marketing Strategist- I help agents package their unique strategy to expand their real estate business*
- *CEO PowerHouse Mortgage*
- *Founder BAWS Inc. -Women's Network*
- *CEO Synergy Escrow Inc*

Proud Mother of 3.5 Children, Married 29 years, God Loving, Grateful, Spirited Soul.

BIC DECARO
Bic DeCaro & Associates EXP Realty
Team Leader & Realtor

CHAPTER 12

Knowing What You Want To Do and the Reason Behind It

with Bic DeCaro

HEY THERE, SUPERWOMEN. I AM SO EXCITED today to have my next guest. We're talking about real estate and you know how much I love real estate—and that I love to talk to amazing women. And lately I have been talking with some of the top realtors in the U.S., and what's especially exciting is hearing their background stories. They are different but they are all inspiring. Now, I was in the real estate industry for a long time, so I'm one of these crazy people who think real estate is sexy. But let's get to my guest, Bic DeCaro, founder of Bic DeCaro & Associates, which is affiliated with eXp Realty.

Q: Bic DeCaro, how are you?
Bic De Caro: I'm doing wonderful. Thank you. How about you, Tam?

Q: I'm excited. You are in the top one percent of real estate agents in Northern Virginia, you have over two decades in the business, and half a billion dollars in sales. You've been enjoying sharing your experience through mentoring and coaching agents. Your team production is crazy. You grew from $38 million to $91 million in just two years. This success is incredible but I want to go back and ask how you even got into real estate.
BD: I've been in real estate for 22 years. I was actually doing sales and sales management, and my brother owned a small boutique brokerage. He saw what I was doing, working for a company, and he said, "You know, with what you're doing, how much you love working with people and the dedication that you put into it, you should really think about launching your own business." And he explained that in real estate you can have your own business, you can work at your own pace—and at the commitment level and the level of work that I was putting in working for another company, he was like, "Imagine if you did that for yourself. The sky's the limit!" And he was right. So that's how I got into it.

Q: So true. You have a husband, you have two kids, you have two dogs. How do you choose to balance your lifestyle around your business?

BD: I always say that my husband married into it, my kids were born into it, my dogs also came into it. So they're used to it. It's harder, I think, sometimes when you are starting something completely new after you have a family. But I did this before I was married and then my kids were born into it. So it developed over time, but I will tell you, there were challenges along the way because of the guilt you have, right? If I am going all in, how can I commit to being the great wife, before kids, and then when I had kids, I was like, how can I do this and also be a really great mom? Do I need to put my career on hold?

But real estate is actually one of the careers that works really well with being able to juggle and balance it all and allowing you to work as much or as little as you want. That said, if you want to grow quickly, you do have to make those sacrifices up front. And because my family didn't know any other way, it was a little bit easier in that sense. The hard part was me changing my mindset and moving away from what I thought was the stereotypical "good wife" and "good mom."

Q: I'm so glad you're bringing this up, because this is something I think that a lot of women can relate to. One of the reasons I loved real estate so much was because there are so many areas that you can go into, so many different things you can do, and you can make it your own. But bringing up just the guilt that we women often face. I think we're socialized into that, where we just have guilt around what we're supposed to do. So what have you been able to create as a result of you working through this and creating a life that you want? What have you been able to do that you wouldn't be able to do in some other careers?

BD: I mean, the amazing thing about it was that if I could organize my calendar and my schedule, I could serve my clients the best that I possibly could and also be there for my family at the same time. I could be there for them at their games, be there at my daughter's performances, and neither side would really know. The sacrifices really came from me getting up earlier or going to bed later, it's these different things, but it didn't have to impact them. And when I saw that I could have it all—I mean, there's certain things that you have to say no to, but overall, in the beginning, when I had super high energy and I was just excited that I was able to do it all. And I was able to do it all, but it does catch up to you.

So as it started catching up to me, the way that I was able to do it is through leveraging people and scaling the business. And it's hard to do when you're a type-A person, which a lot of great realtors are. And I think a lot of women are type-A. We want to be in control. And so what I was able to do is replicate what I was building and that allowed me flexibility to spend time with my family and be able to go on trips with them and then also build the business and really help other people and other women along the way.

I didn't realize this in the beginning, but almost all of my hires early on were women. I didn't really mean to target it that way, but I guess that was what was happening, because it was my understanding of the needs of women. So for four or five years, it was like, if I ever had a man on the team, it was only one at a time. And it wasn't intentional, but it was just understanding what I felt like I needed and I was going through, so I could relate to and empathize with the women that came and worked with me. I could see what they might need, what they needed to build, and I knew that flexibility was important.

Q: I think you're right. It's probably the reason I started doing what I do, working with women. Not because I have anything against men, I just know the needs of women. When you've already figured it out for yourself, you're like, "OK, I know they need this." What have your biggest obstacles been, whether in life or business? Things you've had to overcome that you think will be helpful to other women to hear?

BD: I'm still a work in progress, so I don't know that I've actually overcome it, but I would tell you that I had to work through it and that has helped me. It's mindset, and the fear in our minds that we have, it's not wanting to put ourselves out there. At the beginning of me getting into the business, I was the secret agent. "Secret" agent because I didn't really want people to know. And I'm not really even sure why that was. Maybe it was embarrassment, or I was afraid that if I failed that people would know or judge me. I was fearful of people judging what I was doing, not believing I could do it, or whatever it was. So I was a little bit secretive about what I was doing, and that caused me to grow at a slower pace in the beginning.

It was only after seeing the result of my efforts, my work, and my clients giving me great testimonials and reviews. Those were the validations that I needed. I also hired a coach who helped me. And then I realized later on, it repeated itself again. So if you know your fear and your tendencies, you have to know that it's going to surface again at different times about different things. So I got through being that secret agent, but then the next part was being the secret leader, the secret builder. So I was building a team, but I was fearful of who would want to follow me. Who wants to be on my team? So that started creeping into my mind.

I think this happens to a lot of people. I didn't realize it while it was happening, but when I was building the team, I wasn't really telling people. And, you know, how do you attract people if you're not telling them? And I think it was just a fear in my mind that maybe no one would want to join. I was an agent starting out, so it was, like, maybe no one wants to work with me because I'm new. So those are the things that we tell ourselves. And they are not necessarily true, but we believe them so long as we're telling ourselves that. And I needed to move away from that.

Q: That is so common. I had a call with someone this morning who was going through the same thing. Sometimes we call it limiting beliefs. I was laughing with my husband—we were talking about Elon Musk and how many companies he has started. Now, you know, everybody says he's a genius, but I really think that he just believes in himself. He just comes up with these ideas and goes!

A lot of women are just as smart and creative, but they hold themselves back. So it's really a very common thing that you're feeling. I would bet that most women listening to this podcast are feeling the same way in their business or in their life. So thank you so much for sharing that. You're obviously getting through it because you're building an amazing team, you've done an amazing amount of revenue. What inspires you now?

BD: So for me, I think it really is that when I overcame those things, I was able to build something. I've been fortunate enough to be around many other inspiring women, successful women, and other mentors that led the way. And I feel like I have the opportunity now to be able to inspire others and give back and share my knowledge to help move other people.

Q: That is so good. I can feel that. What would you tell another woman who really wants to be successful? Where should she start?

BD: Understand what it is that you want to do and what is the reason behind it. A lot of people don't even know why they get into certain businesses. You have to understand what it is that drives you. And once you understand that, it will then help you develop it. If you're just jumping from thing to thing, or you're doing it because everybody else is doing it, chances are you're not going to stick with it. It has to be something from within. That's going to be the driver that you're willing to make sacrifices for. So first, get to understand it, and then write down the plan or the goal. Let's say, your short-term goals and then your long-term goals so that you can draft a plan, like a roadmap, to get there.

Without that, you're going to get overwhelmed along the way. When you get to the bumps, when the obstacles come your way, it's easy to give up if you don't have a plan in place. If you have a plan, you can say, "If I just stick to my plan, I'm bound to get through it." But without that plan, you'll start second-guessing everything, you might want to start over, all kinds of stuff. So along with that, get a mentor to help you or hire a coach. Invest in yourself because you're worth it. And I think that's another thing—a lot of times women are willing to do and commit for others, but they don't always do that for themselves.

Q: So true. We think we are somehow not a good woman or good mother if we start asking for help, and that's just not true. I mean, we need to be better delegators. Much better delegators! Bic, I love it. You are in the Northern Virginia area, but do you work with agents all over the U.S.?

BD: Absolutely. Our network, through our capital growth pioneers within eXp, we have agent referrals throughout the country, and we do partner with a lot of other agents that we help with training, masterminding, collaborating, sharing growth ideas, and also just offer referrals back and forth of people relocating in and out of the area. We are always looking for partners, and now even internationally.

Q: Very cool. I have loved this conversation. How can people find you, learn about your team, or connect to ask questions about you or about real estate in general?
BD: I still actually love getting phone calls, so I'm going to give you my email and phone number. My phone number is (703) 395-3662, and my email is bic@bicdecaro.com and those are the best ways to reach me. I'm so glad to be here today and grateful and honored to be chatting with you and sharing a bit with everyone.

Q: I look forward to all the stuff we're going to be doing together and thank you so much for your time.
BD: Thank you.

BIC DECARO

Bic DeCaro is the Team Leader of Bic DeCaro & Associates of eXp Realty, a real estate team that ranks in the top 1% of agents in Northern Virginia. With over two decades in the business and half a billion in sales, Bic enjoys sharing her experience through mentoring and coaching agents. Her team production grew from $38M to $91M in just 2 years.

She is a graduate of the Northern Virginia Association of Realtors Leadership Institute. She chaired NVAR's Community Outreach Committee and the Vietnamese Realtor Forum for several years before starting her team. She has served on Zillow's Agent Advisory Board since 2012 and currently serves on the Board of Directors for Cape Ivy. Bic grew up in McLean, Virginia and received her Bachelor's of Science Degree in Psychology from the

University of Mary Washington. She currently lives in Great Falls, VA with her husband, 2 children and 2 dogs. In her spare time, she enjoys spending time with family and friends, attending her kid's games, traveling, playing tennis and golf.

You have to understand what it is that drives you. And once you understand that, that will then help you develop it.

—*Bic De Caro*

YOU'RE ALWAYS ONE DECISION AWAY FROM A TOTALLY DIFFERENT LIFE

TIME TO BOSSUP!

SECTION 3
Health

GRACE TAN
eXp REALTY LLC, Broker Associate

CHAPTER 13

The light at the end of the tunnel is always there. Keep marching

with Grace Tan

HEY THERE, SUPERWOMEN. I AM SO EXCITED TO have my next guest. A lot of you know that I have years of experience in real estate, and I have always had this thing about property. It's been a lifelong love of mine. And I have been so excited to be talking recently with a lot of impressive women in real estate. Real estate is an amazing field for women, as there are so many ways you can participate in it. There is a new company with an innovative way of doing real estate that I had never even heard of before—it's not your typical broker/realtor relationship and we're going to hear all about it. So, let's get to my guest, who is with eXp Realty New Jersey and New York.

Q: Grace Tan, how are you?
Grace Tan: Hello! How are you, Tam? The honor is mine.

Q: I am so glad to have you. Let's start with how you got into real estate. How did you start down this road?
GT: I need to go farther back in my history—a few steps before I got into real estate. I came to the US for my college. My ethnicity is Chinese, I was born in Malaysia. Let me say first that I'm someone who dares to do things when people say, "Don't do it." Most people do not dare to make changes. They are what I call the "should have, would have, could have," group. **To succeed one should take risks and do the opposite of the naysayers!**

Upon getting my undergrad degree, I was hired as an accountant in the accounting department at the branch of an international European bank based in New York City. I hated the job, but I needed sponsorship to stay in the country. I didn't have much of an option at the time but at the same time I started thinking on how to get out of my situation. Let me first share something with the young ladies (and young men) out there. Never let people define who you are. **It's up to you to define who you are, and what you want to be.**

During my training I was assigned to four different departments to get familiar with the bank's operations: one month per department. In my second month, I was assigned to process tickets in the back-office for the trading floor. This was many years ago, when traders would do deals and the back-office clerks would have to walk up to the traders, get the paperwork, come back to the desk, and input the deals. Now it's all done by technology. (big smile)

I wanted to be a trader after witnessing the excitement and fast pace of the trading floor. However, at the bank, if you don't have advanced degrees like an MBA or a PhD, you are not getting the job. So, it seems that a young inexperienced 23-year-old just out of college with an undergrad degree and a female (trading floor was male dominated and it still is) would have no chance. But I got the job! And this is what I did to earn it. All the traders would get into the office at around 7:30am and the head trader/manager of the trading floor would get in at 7:00am, I would wake up at 5:00am and came to the office and at my desk by 6:00am, study the *Wall Street Journal*, the news on Bloomberg and other reports. Then at 7:00am the head trader/manager would come in, and I would go and knock on his door: "Hi, Ron, can I talk to you?"

At the end of the day, at around 5:30pm, all the traders would leave, the head trader/manager would stay, and I would go back again. "Hi, Ron, can I talk to you about what happened today?" After doing that for over a month, the opportunity came knocking when one of the traders left the company. Seemingly impressed by my thirst for knowledge and energy, I was offered the opportunity to be a junior trader. For me it was surreal, but you know what - I made it happen because I pursued it with all I had! Next thing I knew was I was sitting next to the head trader learning all about trading monetary funds. Here, I started my career as a trader at 23, just graduated with only a bachelor's degree, which had never happened before at the bank! I was the youngest trader on the trading floor to have my own book, the only Asian female trader working alongside male colleagues at the bank.

I worked in the financial industry for many years. When I became a mother, I decided to make a priority shift and that was to spend more time with my son while doing something constructive and meaningful at the same time. Being fluent in Mandarin, I came up with the idea of starting a language school in the town I lived in. It was a way to spend time with my son teaching him and other kids a language in which proficiency was becoming important in the business world. Starting from scratch with no prior experience in the education field, I founded and ran a language school for seven years. I practically did everything, from scouting locations, creating the curriculum, marketing and hiring teachers. This was my foray into entrepreneurship. I really had to hustle every step of the way and the experience was priceless!

But my true love has always been finance and investment. Real estate became my passion because not only does it provide a roof over someone's head, a life necessity, but it is also a vehicle that can provide financial security. To me that is a win win. If one plans strategically, real estate can be a great way to build wealth and provide financial security for them and their family. I utilize my knowledge in investment to assist my clients with their real estate needs and to help them leverage real estate to increase their overall net worth. I always tell my clients, **"You are not just buying a roof over your head, this is also an asset that keeps getting more valuable over time."**

Q: That is so good, because you're looking at someone's home as an investment. As a way for them to build their portfolio, their net worth. I love this. And so you went into real estate, which a lot of women do. A lot of us make these decisions based on our children. But how did you know that real estate was going to be such an interest of yours? You're coming from something completely different.

GT: Well, it is different, but in many ways, it is the same if you think about it. It's all about making good investments. It's all about planning for the long term to build wealth. What I like about real estate is as I said earlier, it is a life necessity – people need a place to live no matter what. And emotionally, a house is also a home where I provide a loving place and shelter for my family, so it provides a lot of sentimental value as well. It is this double whammy if you may build wealth and provide shelter which is so compelling to me.

Q: I do, too. I love that. What have been some of the challenges you have personally had, you know, maybe as a woman in real estate or maybe something in your life that's been difficult?

GT: As a woman, I don't feel I am at any disadvantage or advantage because I see people as human beings. They all work with me, and I want to work with everyone. So, in terms of gender or race, I don't see those things. When something blocks me, I see it as a problem, that's it, and then how I am going to solve it. However, you asked me a very good question. You see me today, so lively, so good. Last year, at the end of February, I had a stroke.

Q: Oh, wow. Was there any lead up to that?

GT: No sign, no warning. Everybody knows how intense

I am. "Grace Tan always hustles, she never stops." That is quite true, I never stop. I'm always moving. I only sleep, like, four hours a day. I wake up at 5:00am, I'll be on the computer, I'll be doing things. A lot of my clients are overseas in Asia so my interactions with them can happen very late at night or in the wee hours of the morning.

Q: Was that caused by stress that you just didn't detect? Or where did it come from?
GT: I had three neurosurgeons all confirmed I had a stroke but none of them could tell me why I had the stroke. I personally think it's this reason: I think I have been living an "unhealthy lifestyle" that I was very much used to, and my body didn't send out any signal until that very moment of crisis. My mind is always on the go. These piled up. Because once you're used to it, you don't recognize that this is unhealthy, right? This year, my goal is to be more mindful of my body and exercise more. I am very strong now; I am very happy to tell you that my doctors said I have fully recovered, and I am as healthy as any healthy person. I have to say the medication that I had to take for my recovery was wreaking havoc on my state of mind. I cried a lot, and I wasn't sure why I was crying. At times, I felt suicidal. For someone who was always optimistic and lively as I was, that was very hard to deal with.

Q: Oh, wow, so you were feeling depressed.
GT: Yes, and being constantly depressed is just excruciating.

Q: Was it a side effect?
GT: Yes, it was a side effect from the medication. I had the stroke during COVID time. My husband worked from

home, and my son's school was at home as well. Like most women, we have that motherly instinct and want to take care of people, we always want to be so strong. This was the very first time in my life that I became muted and passive. I even needed help to get to the bathroom. I felt vulnerable and useless.

It's a liberating feeling for me to reveal what happened to me. It feels good for me to talk about the vulnerable moments in my life. You always want to be strong but when something like this happens, it's okay for others to pick you up and help you. Nothing to be ashamed of. During recovery, I slowed down at work for many months. I am so so touched and humbled that my clients are loyal to me. They waited for me. They said, "Don't worry. Just take care of yourself."

Q: That's so good. I'm so glad you shared that story. Because women, first of all, we often don't think enough about taking care of ourselves. We're taking care of everyone else; we're running around. What is inspiring you now?
GT: What is inspiring me right now is being inspired by my colleagues. These women that I am writing this book with are an amazing bunch! Overall, I am truly truly inspired by how collaborative and supportive my colleagues are. The culture of sharing success to help one another succeed is second to none!

Q: Right. Oh, wow. Yeah. That's amazing. What would you tell another person who was interested in going into real estate? What should they do to be successful?
GT: I would say this. Learn from those who know real estate. Let's say you don't have experience in real estate, but every experience you have in life will help you out and

then you can come to people who have more experience than you are in real estate and learn from them. I joined a new brokerage firm this year, a year after my stroke. I needed a strong comeback. I was looking for a firm with the following criteria: a company with a great collaborative culture, strong partnership globally, ownership in the company, a good healthcare plan, cutting edge technology and providing top service. From that perspective, my current brokerage really stood out. Prior to my stroke, I was already one of the top producers in the areas I covered. In these short six months my production has already exceeded annual production with my previous firms. Agents build great friendships which translates to collaboration. You can't go it alone to be successful. The firm has developed an environment for that kind of support. And you in turn contribute to that support system by sharing your knowledge and experience to help others.

Q: That's awesome. Grace, this has been so good. Thank you for sharing your story.
GT: Thank you for your time, Tam. I really enjoyed this back and forth.

Q: How can someone learn more about you or about real estate? How can they get in touch with you?
GT: I promote my clients' listings in US and international markets. I partner closely with agents in other states in America and internationally. Facebook: GraceTanUSARealtor, Instagram: GraceTanUSARealtor and Wechat: GraceTanUSARealtor. ExpandGlobalProperties, powered by eXp Realty LLC.

Q: I love it. Thank you. I look forward to all the stuff that we are doing together.

GT: Thank you, Tam.

GRACE TAN

Grace Tan has many years of real estate experience representing both residential and commercial. As a top producer, Grace has won many real estate accolades and awards including the prestigious Circle of Excellence. Her clients have raved about her attention to detail, negotiating skills and intimate knowledge of her localities. Her trustworthiness, hard work and ability to bring all relevant parties to close deals have earned Grace repeat business from her clients.

Prior to her career in real estate, Grace worked in Wall Street for many years as a trader where she was responsible for monetary funding. She was also a financial advisor. Grace's in-depth knowledge of corporate and personal finance provide a value-add to her clients looking for investment opportunities.

Grace is a founding member of AREAA Northern Jersey chapter and is appointed to its board of directors. Asian Real Estate American Association (AREAA) is the largest Asian real estate organization in the US with more than 17,000 members. Through her expansive network in the US and global markets, Grace has had great success in assisting sellers and developers connect with qualified buyers.

Grace work closely with her agent partners to assist clients in New Jersey, New York, Florida and beyond. Grace can be reached at Instagram: GraceTanUSARealtor, Facebook: GraceTanUSARealtor or Wechat: GraceTanUSARealtor. Grace is fluent in Mandarin, Cantonese, Fujianese and Malay.

请看下页中文版
Next page for Chinese version

嗨！女强人们，你们好。现在，我要访问下一位嘉宾了，好兴奋！你们之中有许多人都知道，我在房地产方面有多年的经验，我经常都和产业打交道，这已是我毕生的最爱。最近，我同房地产界的许多女中豪杰经常交流，我很是兴奋，对女性来说，房地产是一个很奇妙的领域，你可以通过许多渠道参与其中。我现在的访问的嘉宾是 eXp Realty新泽西州和纽约州 的 Grace Tan陈琼芳女士。

问：我很高兴，能有机会和你聊聊。话题就从房地产开始吧！我很想知道，你是怎么"入行"的？
答：话说从头，让我先回述我"入行"前的那段小史吧！我出生在马来西亚，华裔。中学毕业后负笈美国，攻读本科会计系。自觉性格稍微倔强，别人认为不能为之事，我却偏要不能为而为之，似乎有点"明知山有虎，偏向虎山行"的武松精神。我一向相信"不入虎穴，焉得虎子?"要成功就要不怕冒险！

毕业后，我受雇于纽约一家欧洲银行当一名会计师，受训期为四个月。坦白说，我不很满意这份工作。但我需要一家公司作为我的赞助人，我才可以在美国住下来。当时我虽没有多个选择，但还是千万百计，老想如何才能转入住境。我的座右铭是："活出自己"，我不为别人而活，要煎要炒、要胖要瘦，我的一切由我作主，但愿年轻的朋友们与我共勉。

在受训期间，为着要熟悉银行的运作，我先后被派往四个不同的部门去实习。第二个月我就被派到后勤办公室，处理交易大厅的买卖单据。那时候，从事交易的同事在完成买卖后，单据等文件的文书工作，完全交由后勤文员处理，然后输入电脑。现在，这一切都交由科技去代劳了。

当时我目睹交易大厅的紧张又刺激的营业氛围，渴望自己也能成为一名交易员。但是，在银行工作，如果没有更高的学位，如硕士或博士，你休想得到这个职位。当年我23岁，刚获得学士学位离开学院，没有工作经验，更何况又是一名女性(一直到现在，男性交易员依旧占绝大多数)，但我居然得到了交易员的职位！这是我不懈努力的结果。交易大厅的主管龙先生，早上七点便到办公室，所有的交易员则在半小时后的七点半左右才抵步。而我呢？凌晨五点钟就起身了，六点钟便已经坐在办公室的位子上了，先读读《华尔街时报》、《彭博社》的资讯和其他的报导。七点钟主管"驾到"，我会走去他的办公室叩门："早安，龙先生，我可以同你谈谈吗？"下午五点钟左右，所有交易员都下班了，但主管还留下。我会再去他的办公室，说："龙先生，我可以同你谈谈今天发生的事情吗？"

这样的工作我做了一个多月之后，机会来了！有一位交易员离开公司。主管好像赏识我的好学心态和旺盛精力，擢升我为初级交易员。这对我固然宛如美梦一般，其实是我不遗余力的耕耘果实。此后，我跟着主管尽量学习关于金融交易的一切。千里之行，始于跬步，以23岁的年龄、凭借一个学士学位，我开始了我的事业。在这银行是史无前例的。在交易大厅，我是最年轻的、独立自主的交易员，也是在银行里与男同事"同捞同煲"的唯一亚洲女性。

我在金融领域工作多年，当我初为人母时，我决定优先照顾家庭，花较多的时间陪我的儿子，但同时也做一些有建设性和有意义的事情。我熟谙中文和普通话，于是萌生了在我居住的镇上开一间语文学校的念头。这样一来，我就有时间和我的儿子在一起，教导他和别的孩子多学会一种在商场上日益重要的语文。在教育方面，我毫无经验，一切只能从零开始。实际上，以物色地点、招聘教师、编排课程到寻找生源......等，我无所不包。这是我涉足企业的起点，尽管步履蹒跚，我还是一步一脚印走了过来的，那经验是无价的！

但是，一直以来，金融与投资都为我所爱。房地产之所以成为我的最爱，那是因为它不只是让人有瓦遮头，也提供金钱增值的保障。这是双赢的买卖。如果规划周详，房地产也是一条生财之道，能给人们带来稳妥的财富安全。我以我的投资知识，在房地产方面，尽力帮助客户满足他们之所需。我经常告诉我的客户："你买的不只是一间房屋，而是价值与日俱增的资产"。

问：好极了，你把置业当作是一种投资。我喜欢以这种方式建立他们的投资组合，也就是他们的资产净值。你因此投入了房地产这一行，很多女性也都这样做。我们之中很多人做出这个决定，主要的考量是我们的孩子。但你怎么知道房地产这一行对你的好处呢？你毕竟来自完全不同的行业。

答：的确不一样，但你仔细一想，就看出大同小异了。它们都在做良好的投资，也都是累积财富的长远之计。正如我早前说过的，我爱房地产这一行，是因为人们生活的需要。不管怎样，每个人都需要一处栖身之所。从感情上说，一间屋就是一个家———一个庇护全家大小的"爱巢"，它的价值是无与伦比的。

问：你我可谓是"英雄所见略同"。身为房地产界的一名女性，你遭遇过也许是你一生中难以应付的挑战吗？

答：男女都是人，我不觉得我处于什么劣势或优势。他们和我风雨同舟、携手共济、合作愉快。我不在乎性别，也看不见肤色。在遇到阻碍时，我当作是一个问题，设法解决就是了。总之，你问了我一个极好的问题。今天，你看我蹦蹦跳跳，好活泼！你可能不知道，去年二月秒,我有过一次中风。

问：啊！怎么会那样呢？

答：没有征兆，没有预警。大家常夸我向来做事一丝不苟，从不马虎，总是停不下来。"琼芳Grace一直都很忙，她停不下来"。这是实话，我真的停不下来。我一直在动，有时一天只睡四小时。我早上五点起床，然后上电脑工作，或是做别的事情。我的许多客户是居住在美国之外的其他国家，只有在很晚或凌晨的时候，我才能同他们互动。

问：是不是这些压力导致你中风，而你并不察觉。究竟是从何而来呢？

答：三位神经外科医生都已证实我的确中风，但没有一位能告诉我，我为什么会中风？我自己猜想的原因是：我早已习惯的、不健康的生活方式。我的身体没有发出任何讯号，中风说来就来。我的头脑一直很忙碌，积年累月，一旦习以为常，便无法认出这样的生活方式是不健康的，对吗？今年，我要更照顾我的健康和做更多的锻炼。现在，我很硬朗，我乐于告诉大家，我的医生说，我已经完全痊愈了！我和健康的人一样健康！我不得不说，药物治疗当初的确颠覆我的心理状态。我哭过很多次，但我真的不知道我为什么哭？我有时想到自杀。对于像我过去那样乐观和活跃的人，这种情况很难处理。

问：噢，你因此感到沮丧吧？
答：是的，我经常沮丧，糟透了。

问：这是副作用吗？
答：是的，这是药物治疗的副作用。我是在新冠疫情时中风的。我的先生在家工作，我儿子的学校也在家里。和多数的妇女一样，我的母性本能总是要我照顾好家人。我们常常都要这样强壮。这一次，是我有生以来的第一次，变成了哑口无言和极其被动。我甚至需要家人搀扶走进浴室。我觉得我弱不禁风，毫无用处。

把我中风的经历公开了，我感觉到"全身松晒"。让你们知道我一生中弱不禁风的时刻，对我来说是美事一椿。我想通了，我一路来要当女强人，但当发生这样的不幸事件时，让人予我一臂之助没什么不对，没什么可耻的。在复元期间，有好多个月我放慢了我的工作步伐。在那段漫长的日子里，我的客户对我不离不弃，令我感动不已。他们等我复元后养好身子，他们说："别担心，你要先照顾好你自己"。

问：好极了。我很高兴分享这个故事。首先，我们女人对于照顾自己总是想得不够周到。我们东奔西走。现在是什么鼓舞着你？
答：现在是公司的同事们鼓舞着我。和我合写这本书的诸位同事，确实是了不起的团伙。千真万确，正是同事们的群策群力与通力合作，给予我巨大的鼓舞。同事之间休戚与共的无间关系，在我们公司里是独一无二的文化。

问：噢！太好了。假定有人很想加入房地产这一行，你会对他说什么？他该怎么做才会成功？

答：我会这样说。你要向懂得房地产的人学习。你没有房地产的经验，但你的生活经验会帮助你，然后向更有房地产经验的人请教，向他们学习。我在今年加入新公司，那是我中风的一年后。我必须以强劲的势态卷土重来。我心仪的公司必须具有这些准则：合作互助的文化，全球性的坚强夥伴，良好的医疗保健计划，分享公司的拥有权而不纯是一位职员，先进科技和提供于客户一流的服务。从这个观点来看，我现在的公司确实是首选。加入之前，我在我所经营的地区，已经是最佳的营业员之一。我在我现在的公司大约六个月，这半年的营业额，已超越我过去每一家公司的年度营业额。公司有很强的互助文化。经纪人情同手足、相互提携，发挥集体的智慧和力量，这是我们所信赖的。单兵独马不可能成功。我们拓展了这种互相支援的环境。彼此之间以知识和经验交互分享，就是对这个互助体制的贡献。

问：棒极了！琼芳 Grace，这太好了。谢谢你让我分享你的故事。

答：谢谢你的访问。

问：如果有人要知道更多关于你，关于房地产的资讯，该怎么联络你？

答：我在美国和国际上推广销售我的客户房源。我也与美国其他州的房地产经纪人和国际伙伴密切合作。微信：GraceTanUSARealtor。脸书：GraceTanUSARealtor。Instagram：GraceTanUSARealtor。Grace Tan。ExpandGlobalProperties，由 eXp Realty LLC 提供支持。

When you don't
see the light at the
end of the tunnel,
you keep marching
until you see it. It is
always there.

—*Grace Tan*

VERONICA FIGUEROA
The Figueroa Team
Chief Visionary Officer

CHAPTER 14

Being Crystal Clear of What Success Looks Like in Your Life

with Veronica Figueroa

HEY THERE, SUPERWOMEN. I AM SO EXCITED TO have my next guest. Everyone by now knows I love real estate, I love amazing boss ladies doing big things in real estate, and my next guest is no exception. She is an amazing realtor down in Orlando, Florida, where she leads an award-winning team. Inman, the real estate media and events company, has named her team the Most Innovative Team of the Year and she has been an Inman Influencer since 2016. That's just a small sample of the recognition she has received. A lot of women in the real estate game look up to her. So I'm honored to have this time to find out what makes her tick, why she went into real estate, and all the questions.

Q: Veronica Figueroa, how are you?
Veronica Figueroa: I'm good. Thank you for having me, I'm super excited to be here. Thank you for uplifting other women and bringing us together.

Q: Yes. It's funny you said that, because one of the things you've written is that your true passion has always been to inspire and help others with directional wisdom, to help them follow their dreams. And I feel like that was part of my road as well. I really wanted to inspire people. So how did fulfilling your passion lead you to real estate? Take us on that journey.
VF: I got my real estate license right out of college. A friend of mine had been exploring getting his real estate license, I had just graduated from college, and I had not landed the job that I wanted. I had a background in human resources, and I still hadn't found my career of choice. Human resources was really my passion, because I loved working with people. I always knew I wanted to help develop people and help place them where they wanted to be. That was the goal.

But my friend was like, hey, we should get into real estate, everybody says that if you go into timeshares, you're going to be rich. I was not interested, but he said, "You're not working anyway. What's another certification or license? You can add it to your resume." So I thought, "Actually, that's not a bad idea." I went to real estate class at age 20 and got my license in 2001. He never passed, by the way. That was always an inside joke.

I actually got my real estate license the day after 9/11 and I thought, nobody's going to buy real estate now. Little did I know that we were about to enter one of the biggest booms in the housing market. But in any case, I wasn't focused on that. I still wanted my career in human resources, so I put my real estate license on a shelf. I stored it away. I had tried timeshares, and absolutely did not like it. But then I ended up working, ironically, in the human resources department of a timeshare company.

So I got to work closely with the marketing team and the sales team and learn how they qualify people. I learned a lot. I watched them, I observed, I was part of the initial hiring process. I got to see all these sales reps come in. Fast forward, I'm 25 years old, I'm going through a divorce, I need to supplement my income, and I remembered I had a real estate license. And that real estate license was going to help me supplement my income so that my children wouldn't feel the financial impact of my divorce. If I wanted to put them in private school, if I wanted to do something, I needed to figure out how I was going to make extra money.

I started doing real estate part-time in the residential area, starting off with friends and family. My mom was my first client—shout out to my mom! I always tell the story that I lost my first client's $1,000 deposit, and that happened to be my mom. Since then, I've retired, so she has forgiven me for that. But I started helping friends, I started helping family, I learned a lot and I found myself hiding underneath the desk at my regular job. I thought, "Man, I'm really enjoying helping these families. Imagine if I could do this full time without having to divide myself between this and my safe career. But I love this career, this is what I wanted to do." But I realized that in human resources, people have a long career, so unless they were retiring or, God forbid, passed away, they weren't going anywhere. So the ladder for me to move up looked high. I was going to have to work really, really hard to only *maybe* make it, right?

I thought, "What if I just try this real estate thing full time? And if I absolutely love it, I thrive. If I don't, I can always fall back on my career." My first quarter, I made $17,000 in one month. It all closed. So I was like, I'm rich. I learned quickly that I was not. But I realized I could afford to take care of my kids if I could make this kind of money and then double my efforts. So I quit my full-time job and I went all in. My first full year in real estate, I sold 56 homes. That was 18 years ago and I've never looked backed.

Q: Wow. You know, some people just seem to get in and go right from the start. Do you think you had a knack for it? What was the secret to your success?

VF: I had so many reasons why I needed to succeed. I was a mom, my kids were little, I was going through a divorce. I met a guy that I absolutely love, and I've been married to him now for 16 years. When I married him, he had three kids. So I had a family that I really needed to help provide for while still having balance.

But my success, I think, also goes back to my origin story. My mom was an entrepreneur. She was someone who, when my dad was stationed at a military base, and there were no Latino products or Latino stores in the area, she kind of became the dealer. She was the one who would go to Atlanta, Miami, New York, or Chicago to get the products that you would find in your country or that were culturally connected to you. She would travel to those cities, bring all the products back, and sell them to the Latino community. If there was any little Latino community, she found them and she brought the community together. So she was the OG of me seeing entrepreneurship. I mean, I was selling icees out my door when I was little with my brother. My brother was older than me but he was my assistant. We'd sell icees on a hot summer day to all the kids out playing.

My mom used to make me work for a pair of sneakers. And I'll never be mad at her for that because she taught me this work ethic. So my mom created this persona and then she ended up opening the first bodega in places like Junction City, Kansas, or Columbus, Georgia, where there wasn't a lot of diversity. And I had to work in her store, so I was taught work ethic at a really young age. I was taught community at a really young age.

I also watched my mom become a niche marketer, and I did the same thing when I first started out. I served my Latino community because I was like, well, that's what I am. And I thought that's what I would attract. So for me, my success is a combination of grit, what I witnessed with my parents being hard workers and how they made me work for what I'd wanted.

It was also due to my life changing by being 16 and pregnant. I could have gone the opposite way, but I saw my parents work so hard. I looked them in the eyes and I said, "I'm going to make you proud. I know that this wasn't part of the plan, but I am going to make you proud." I still went to college—with my kid—I graduated in the same time. I just had this work ethic that had been instilled in me ever since I was little, and I carried that into anything that I did. Including when I hit the ground running in real estate. I don't know how to do anything small. It's all gas, no brakes. There's no in between. It's all or nothing.

Q: **You saw what needed to be done and you just put the pedal to the metal and made it happen, no excuses. I love that. What are some of the challenges you have experienced in your business? As a female, as a woman of color, as a Latina, a mom, you know, just all these things that we have to go through?**

VF: I'm super proud of what I've accomplished. We are the number-one team in the world for eXp.

Q: Amazing.

VF: I'm the first woman in this company to ever sell more than 2,100 homes in one year, to lead a team the size that I lead, to build an organization the size we did. And I am so proud of a lot of the firsts that we've done. I sit on Zillow's Advisory Board. I sit in boardrooms that I never thought someone like me would be in. I feel like I have been blessed in so many ways that I want to continue to extend a chair at that table and help people get here. But a lot of people don't know everything that has happened behind the scenes.

I have struggled with a lot of things, but now that I have this deep understanding of gratitude for the journey of life, I am grateful for all of it because otherwise I wouldn't be who I am today. I've struggled with mental health. I've struggled with depression. I've struggled with abuse. I've struggled with alcoholism. I've struggled with betrayal. I went through a divorce. I've seen my kids—I thought I was providing them a wonderful life because my success came with a financial reward, but it was at the cost and the sacrifice of me being a "workaholic" and neglecting some of the motherly duties that I wish I could get a do over on, right? My kids are now adults, and we talk a lot and they see my world and they respect and love me. They're inspired by what I did, but back then all they knew was their mom was always working.

So I had to overcome a lot of challenges. My marriage was not in a good place. Maybe I wasn't cheating on my husband, but I was cheating on him with my career. I was so sought-after. I was doing big things and I also wanted to just prove something to someone. But that someone was myself, the little girl in me. The little girl in me that needed validation that I was somebody, that I am seen.

Of course I talk about my work ethic being insane because my parents taught me well. But that also brought me a lot of challenges because when most kids were enjoying their lives, I was working. I was chasing this idea that money was a reward. I was programmed to believe that if I give you something, you'll like me. So I would work more to buy my friends a gift or buy that guy a gift. Those were patterns that I didn't realize were going to flow into my adulthood, because I really was dealing with deep-rooted trauma that I didn't realize or recognize. So all of that flowed into my adulthood.

What was my addiction? My work was my addiction. Eventually, when I would deal with depression or other issues—in my industry, it's very easy to get caught up in the cocktails, in the networking—I was the one who would shut it down. Like I said, all gas, no brakes, I would have the last vodka in my hand. It was not a pleasant sight. I am proud to say that I am now a year and a half sober. I don't drink anymore, I don't need it. But there was an era in my life where I was just hiding all of my trauma with success. Everything was piling up until I just imploded. I dealt with weight gain. I've had the gastric sleeve and bypass for repair because my body rejected it and I was dealing with GERD that could turn into cancer in my esophagus, and my acid reflux.

My weight got so out of control because of my obsession with success. When I looked in the mirror, I was 100 pounds overweight. My marriage was falling apart. My kids were falling apart. I had people in my business that were supposedly friends who were betraying me. I was working to just keep the lights on, barely thrive, at one point in my career. But as long as I won an award, that was all that mattered. So as you ask me what trials and challenges I've overcome, you pick which one you want, but I will quote you this: It's all been part of the journey.

I have, since then, been able to live a life of accountability. I have a mental health coach, I have a soul coach, I have a business coach. I have a life by design that absolutely makes me want to, now that I look back on everything that I've overcome, just go back and hug my younger self because she's overcome so much. And I remember what it felt like walking in my darkest days to now living in pure bliss and joy because I was willing to acknowledge the areas of my life that needed to be addressed.

I have been able to lose 80 pounds and keep the weight off. I'm healthy. I'm happy. My husband and I renewed our vows. My kids are, for the most part, thriving. My business is doing well and I'm working less, but I'm making more of an impact. And when I say I work less, I don't have to exchange my time for money because now it's my experience, my expertise, that is the value I bring. I now know I'm worthy.

Before, I used to think I needed to prove that I deserved people's attention. Now, I live a completely different life. It's all about alignment. It's all about purpose. It's all about impact. The abundance will follow. So overcoming health issues, marriage issues, mental health, financial betrayal, you name it, I probably have walked that path. I don't talk about that every day, but I'm not afraid to share it. I think we all have a story. We've all had to overcome something. Real estate is just the vessel that allows me to connect with other people that, maybe, are overachievers, that have had a career change or have had to make it to balance their family, and then they get sucked into the industry.

I want to now be an advocate for not sacrificing your family to be successful in real estate. You don't have to lose yourself to win or to be a leader in this industry. You don't have to be competitive, you don't have to be cutthroat. You don't have to be drunk. The most dedicated, the most committed and balanced, can have a thriving life. Because why do we do this? We do this to build a life for the people that we love, and to enjoy it. But I did it the wrong way for a long time.

Q: I love how authentic you are. You came through the fire and you lived to share, and you share from a place that's so loving and so giving because you get it. Anyone who hears your story would just be inspired to see what their life could look like on the other side of the struggle. So first I would like to say thank you so much for being that open and authentic. This is the part I love about what I do, just getting a chance to take what you've learned and then fill someone else up with it. And fill me up. Because you just filled me up quite a bit from your story. I thank you for that. What would you tell another woman she should focus on first if she's looking at your success and she wants to get there too? Can she get there without sacrificing so many things?

VF: What a great question. I can't say I have the right answer for everyone, but I can tell you what I would do differently. That's one of the things that my coach taught me. We often ask people, "How did you get where you are?" But what's really a key question is "What would you do differently?" I think I would've invested in loving myself more early on. I've said this before—saying nice things to myself. I think investing in your inner healing is a really important thing before you go out there. If you're struggling with anything and you want to be successful—even if you don't have a drug, alcohol, party story, or traumatic story—just simply speaking nice things to yourself is very important. You don't have to have had a traumatic story.

Prepare yourself for what success looks like in your mind before you experience it, as if you were already living it. What does it taste like? What does it feel like? What does it smell like? Who are the people? Whether you see their faces or not, what is the energy they exude? Because when you start walking the path of success, it will feel different, and there will be challenges that come along with it. But when you have the mental peace of knowing why you're doing this and you already envision what the outcome is going to be without being tied to the outcome but falling in love with the journey.

Whether it's smiling faces, whether it's what that moment of winning and achieving feels like from a good place. It's never about beating someone else. I think you really have to work on what that looks like. So when you have distractions or deterrents or anything that might feel like defeat, just go back to that beautiful feeling of "Yes, I know what it feels like, I know what it's going to smell like, I know what the most beautiful day of my life, when everything is in alignment, feels like, looks like, and I am going after that. My marriage, my health, my wealth, my friendships." If I would've learned that exercise early on, I think I would've been a little bit different, not in a bad way or in a good way, but I just might have been able to experience things a little differently.

So just say nice things to yourself and prepare yourself for success. The days that are going to feel hard, because you committed to what that life on the other side of success looks like, those are the days that you have to go back to that thought and to that mindset and say, "Not today. I'm not quitting today. I know I don't want to make that phone call, I know it's hot outside, I know I just got in a fight with my spouse. Or something just happened that I wasn't expecting and it just is boiling my blood. But I am committed to what I set out to do."

Success is not always going to be rosy every day. It's going to feel hard sometimes. It's going to be challenging. You're going to cry sometimes, you're going to feel totally surprised with the unexpected, the good and the bad, when you're not going to see that competitor coming or something. But just remember that this is your journey. What does success look like for you? You get to write that story. You get to run your own race.

But if I were to give anyone advice who's thinking about what success looks like, you first have to get super crystal clear on what it looks like in your life. And stay so committed to it, to that feeling, to that goal, to that life on the other side of it, that no matter what comes your way, on the other side of it, when you come out, you're going to be like, I cannot believe I was able to walk through that. But I am so grateful that I stayed committed to it.

Q: So good. What is inspiring you right now? You've done so many things, you've accomplished so much in your life. But what is keeping you going?

VF: In the great words of J-Lo, I'm just getting started. She's so inspiring. But I feel like I still got a lot of work to do. I haven't impacted enough lives. I haven't helped grow enough leaders. I haven't helped create enough millionaires yet. It's not even about the money, the overall goal is to impact people's lives. And for a long time, I thought it was local, my team. Then I was introduced to this opportunity at eXp and I can expand globally. We are now in multiple countries: Puerto Rico, Dominican Republic, Colombia, Italy, we just brought in the broker from Dubai. We have partners in India, in different parts of the world now.

But I realize that I'm being selfish if I don't bring my gifts and talent to people in the mainland, in the U.S., the opportunity of what we've been able to build. We have built one of the strongest real estate teams that this industry has ever seen, led by a female, led by a Latina. I lead a pretty diverse group. I'm ready to expand the Fig Team nationally. We've already identified a couple different cities because we've identified who we want to make an impact on and build around them.

So now we're super excited to take our team on an expansion tour and identify leaders that we are going to turn into rock stars in their world and change their world from a leadership capacity to an authority, a thought leader, to changing other people's lives and duplicating a lot of what we've done. I'm on a mission to impact more lives. Not just women, not just Latinos. I want to impact leaders. I want to help unleash leaders that just haven't had an opportunity. They may be sitting idle but they're just one relationship away from changing the rest of their life. I want to be that person for the right people. For the right people, I'm willing to invest my time, my resources, my connections with them, because they have a mission to make an impact on people's lives. So it has to be aligned with that.

I retired from my parents when I started, so just being able to enjoy them and enjoying life with my husband. We just renewed our vows after 18 years and we are madly in love with each other. He and I both want to impact people's lives. We want to show people that you can be a miracle love story. When we came together, we didn't have the right foundation. It was hard. It was a blended family. But through doing the work, both of us, we're really proud to hopefully be what would be considered a miracle of saving your marriage, working on yourself. So we really want to work on helping couples be healthier and more united together and treat themselves with the respect that they were meant to have. Together, that's our passion project—impacting people because we have people who have impacted our lives and we want to give that forward.

We love buying real estate, buying lots of investments and helping build our investment portfolio. I just started a chapter called Grid, which is an investment wealth-building network, and we want to empower people to build wealth through investments. We're educating Black and brown and Latino and diverse groups that maybe are not familiar with what the investment space looks like, and that they can invest in these big multi-family buildings and be in syndications with other financially prepared entities or leaders and own a piece of the buildings and own the block.

Also, I'm really focused on women's empowerment. Working on some retreats with women for a whole, complete transformation: mindset, relationships, health, wealth, and really getting them to boss up, right? To boss up in their business, but also boss up in their life. You cannot be a boss of business and not have your personal life taken care of. What is happening privately will show up publicly. I am a walking testament to that. I could have everything, but if shit's not right at home, it's going to show up. So I really want these women's retreats to be about getting centered, getting honest with your business but also the business of you. Then you can fix everything else around you.

When I stopped drinking, when I stopped eating bad, when I started working on my mental health and my marriage, I thought I was embarking on fixing just my personal life. And that is the year that I ended up selling 2,100 homes and building the number-one team in the world for eXp. I believe it's because I decided to build the business of my life and to fix me first. Then everything else was just organically impacted and it was a beautiful story of watching the people around me also elevate and lead and rise up. So for me, it's all about getting you right first, and then everything else falls into place.

Q: Yes. I love it. I'm so inspired by your story and what you've been through and how many people you're trying to impact. Is there anything else that you would like to share with my audience? I think you represent the possibility, being a woman, a Latina, a mom, with all of this great success, but also working on yourself to the point where you're able to realize the importance of the whole journey. It's not just making the money. Anything else you'd like to share?
VF: If you're reading this, it's probably because you have an interest in real estate or you're in real estate, and I'm here to tell you that you can thrive in any real estate market, as

long as you put in the work. I always say that my actions determine my economy. I've been through multiple shifts in the market, and I just made a decision that I was going to thrive in any market, and that my actions would outperform any interest rate, any inventory crisis, any competitor that comes to the market.

So I'm here to tell you, you can have a thriving real estate career if you put in the work. Accountability is so important. How you run your business is going to be determined by how you run your calendar, how you run your database, and the amount of attempts of conversations that you're going to have. More conversations equal more conversions.

If you ever want to learn more about how we built a team and how we hold our agents accountable and how I landed thousands and thousands of listings, I'm always just a phone call away. Or you can reach me on IG @veronicafigueroainspires, where you can DM me. I'll even give my cell phone: (407) 301-9574. I am super excited to hopefully be someone that can continue to show women that we have a place in real estate, not just that we sell more homes, but we run really strong business organizations and real estate empires.

Q: Thank you so much, Veronica. I cannot wait for all the things that we're going to be doing this year together. **VF:** You're amazing. Thank you.

VERONICA FIGUEROA

Veronica Figueroa is an award-winning Real Estate influencer, keynote speaker, known for her vivacious personality. Veronica leads the #1 Team for Homes Sold in EXP - The Figueroa Team. She regularly engages with other team leads to share her unique techniques that fuel her teams' success. As a result, the Figueroa Team continues to scale and grow as one of the nations' leading teams serving 2,000+ families and clients in 2021 and over 646 million in sales volume.

Veronica has sat on Zillows Advisory Board since 2016. She has been named an Inman Influencer, and in 2017, The Figueroa Team won The Most Innovative Team of the Year by Inman for their bold partnership with the I-Buyer movement and Instant Offers. As a Keynote Speaker, Veronica has shared the stage with many influencers, with one of her highest achievements being her most recent interview with Venus Williams at eXpcon 2021.

Veronicas' true passion is to inspire and help others with directional wisdom and to amplify their communication, connection and confidence to run a successful real estate business. She mentors with passion, guiding her clients to effectively strengthen and elevate their leadership vision to new heights. She will inspire you to take action and become the leader you were always meant to be!

I want to continue
to extend a chair at
the table and help
people get there.

—*Veronica Figueroa*

JENNIFER MAHER
Grit Assist, CEO

CHAPTER 15

Putting Together a Core Habit that Enables Productivity

with Jennifer Maher

HEY THERE, SUPERWOMEN. I AM SO EXCITED today to talk to my next guest. We've been having such a good time connecting with some of the amazing women in real estate for our book, and I've said over and over again that I love real estate. I find real estate sexy, and I love talking to women in real estate. You can go in so many different directions, which is really very cool and makes it so interesting. It's also a great industry to go into if you're a mama. It'll never go out of style. Real estate is one of the most important decisions a person makes in their life. It's your home, shelter for your family. Our next amazing guest is Jennifer Maher. I want to find out how she went from successfully building her team in real estate and doing business all over the world to then launching her new business, Grit Assist, which is a coaching and virtual assistant company. I love that name.

Q: Jennifer Maher, how are you?

Jennifer Maher: I'm good. Yes, Grit Assist is my coaching and virtual assistant company, separate from my real estate business—although it's also related to real estate, of course. I got into real estate honestly, as an uneducated woman who wound up single and pregnant at 27. My mom had been in real estate very briefly when I was younger. And she said, "Well, why don't you get into real estate?" I was in the restaurant business—which is how you end up single and pregnant at 27. So I went for it.

I got out of the restaurant business, because you have to get out of it if you're going to be a mom. It's a lot of nights and craziness. I was doing catering and real estate and I quickly grew to hate catering. It was nothing like the restaurant business. The restaurant business is fun, catering is not. So I did really well as a part-time real estate agent and I was able to be with my daughter, Olivia, who's now 26 and has her own baby. She had asthma and I needed to be around. So I quickly discovered that I could do it all in this industry because it was easy if you learned how to structure your time. It wasn't easy until I really mastered that, but if you structure your time correctly, you can really be present for your family and make money. And honestly, I wasn't educated—besides being able to cook—to make the kind of money doing anything else that I've been able to make in this industry.

Q: I love this. Now with EXP Commercial you have your own successful book of commercial real estate sales business as well as you work with your Licensed daughter Olivia on residential. So a lot of people want to know how you did that! So let's start there. First of all, there are not a lot of women in commercial real estate.

JM: No. Which is the plus. I was doing sales. I've always been attracted to the leadership side of the business, so in 2011 or so I came on board as a partner with J. Philip Real Estate and my job was to open up an office in Putnam County and a commercial division. But I said, nope, it has to be a separate company, so we opened up a separate commercial company and I did both. I had this thriving residential office of which I was the team leader, and I founded the commercial company and we did pretty well. But it was mostly my book of business. I don't know, I just have that kind of drive naturally.

And honestly, in the last 10 plus years, all I've been working on is self-development and really coming into my stride just now, at 51. But I've always had that natural drive and I think that's easy when you are a single mom—a true single mom and there's no father in the picture, which I was for my first daughter. I always say that I had an advantage because I didn't have a choice. I wanted to break the cycle for my daughters and I wanted to create opportunity for them. I didn't even know that I could go to college. I didn't know it was an option when I was at that age. And so I wanted to just create different opportunities and that was always my driving force and my why.

Q: Well, you helped grow a company from a one-room office with 30 associates to three market centers with close to 100 associates. You're kind of a beast!

JM: Yes. It's funny, because I went through this long journey and then I actually stepped into the COO role when the pandemic started. So yes, I was definitely one of the driving forces behind that growth. When I came on board with J. Philip Real estate, I really solidified the systems and the practices. I actually became what's called an implementer when I came into that COO role.

And then through this process, I got back into coaching. A lot of us in real estate share a coach, Jon Cheplak. Through that, I had this self-actualization happen. And while I love J. Philip Real Estate, it is really my partner's baby. It is named after him. I have now stepped down from the COO role and have since parted ways with the company. I finally realized that I've always done it for everybody else. I joined EXP so I could grow in other countries and states and launched Grit Assist, which is really bringing to life what inspires me, which took me 50 years of my life to really understand, to discover that my why is deeper than doing for everybody else. While it's beautiful for a mother to do for her children, and that certainly can help you level up, I have come to this place of realizing what I deserve and being the best version of me and putting my needs first and doing things that inspire me and drive me. That's where I am at this at this point.

J. Philip is always going to be super important to me, and I will always be grateful for the opportunity and growth it brought me at a time where I needed it most. But now I will be working on building eXp in the Dominican Republic, building my commercial client base while supporting my daughter in our residential practice and growing Grit Assist, so a lot of exciting stuff is going on. But I love what you said in the beginning, because not everybody understands real estate and being in a position of leadership. I see it over and over. People come in and they try to compare themselves with agents that everyone can see, the top producers. Veronica Figueroa is a really good example. She will give so much of the credit to the people underneath her. And she's not just saying that. She realizes like I do that there are so many different roles that need to be filled in this industry to make it work.

The failure rate is so high because people are like, "Oh, I can't be Veronica Figueroa." Who can, right? Or "I can't be a Daniel Beer," or whoever—these top, top, top people. They're less than 5 percent of the industry. So a lot of the production comes from other roles, roles that need to be mastered, quite frankly. And even for me, even though every time I put my mind to it, I was able to become a top producer in my market, it's not what I enjoyed. I enjoy coaching and helping others grow. So there really is a spot for everybody in this industry, every personality profile, whatever your strengths, whatever your weaknesses, as long as you have a team leader, a coach, or someone who knows how to place you in your strengths.

Q: Awesome. Tell me a little bit about Grit Assist. It is brand new. What is your vision for it?
JM: It's been morphing. This is pretty fresh, pretty new. I've had virtual assistants in the Dominican Republic for quite some time. I've been working on my residency there. As a single mom I bought and paid off my beachfront dream home in the Dominican Republic as part of a seven-year

plan, which I started about 10 years ago. Now I'm married, and my husband went through a lot of health issues and I just knew I needed to get both of us out of the grind. And so I started working toward what I could do in the Dominican Republic that could bring us some income so that we could live a little easier. That's how it started.

First I was going to do just a full-out virtual assistant company, then I realized I'm not super inspired by that. What I came to realize in this past year is that what makes me alive, what makes me understand my purpose, who I'm meant to be and what exactly I'm meant to do (not that I've filled that role out quite yet, because we're always growing and self-actualizing) is helping people grow, get unstuck, get to the next level.

And then I realized one of the things that I've seen over and over again, because I've been doing coaching for 13 years at this point, is people that get into coaching, they get all excited, then they go to roll out and implement what they've learned and they hit a roadblock. They have no one holding their hand or they don't have the time or capital to invest in what they've learned. This is a tricky market because you're running around like a crazy person with buyers and you're like, I have no more time to take on or do anything new or anything different.

So Grit Assist is for agents, team leaders, and brokers to not only have the coaching, the strategies, and the systems they need, but to immediately have the support at a very affordable rate to help them implement and roll out what they are getting from this coaching program. Because I think the ratio is probably pretty similar. Probably 95 percent of people fail even though they've invested in a coach because of the implementation.

Q: Because of the implementation. That's right.

JM: So Grit Assist is an idea to bridge that gap, that integrity gap between what somebody knows they're capable of, what they want, and then actually taking the steps to get there.

Q: Amazing. What are some of the difficulties you've gone through as you've been building this business? You've been doing this for a while, you're a former single mom, you're a woman in commercial real estate, I'm sure there was a lot.

JM: Commercial real estate was the easiest of all for me because I loved it. I got bored easily with the residential side, going up against the same people with very little challenge. It just didn't excite me. But the commercial aspect, it's unlimited and varied. And I got into commercial real estate the year that I got divorced and I made the most money in a year than ever before. I had done a huge commercial transaction where I got both sides of the deal and I was like, "Great!" Then the market crashed after the divorce and I'm like, "Okay, now what?" And the phone didn't ring.

I was the chairwoman of the local chamber of commerce at that point. And I looked at, "What is my sphere of influence?" And my sphere of influence was business owners and elected officials and they weren't going anywhere. So I had just done that transaction, and I thought, "Okay, let me get into commercial." That was it. I loved it because it's different. You get to use a side of your brain that you don't usually use, you're solving problems and getting creative. I love zoning, investment formulas and development, all the aspects of it. So that was always easy.

But really the biggest challenges were overcoming myself

and my own dark side. It was coming to embrace my weaknesses and get into my strengths and then put together core habits that enabled me to be productive on a much higher level. It's still a challenge, it's always a challenge. But in a lot of ways, the industry has been pretty easy for me. I always hit the ceiling and then I think, okay, I don't want to just go up. I always want to go broader. I want to go wide. That's probably my biggest challenge is I want to branch out this way or that way instead of continuing to go up. But I've enjoyed that process very much. And now I'm ready to go up!

Q: Now you're ready to go up! Of course.
JM: Yes, at 51.

Q: What would you tell another woman who wants to get in this business or start her own business? What should she think about to be successful?
JM: Well, if you're in real estate, definitely break past that wall that you're either residential or commercial. All my commercial friends were so jealous through the pandemic, so jealous when the residential market blew up. But really when I got into the commercial side, what I was able to do was be very client-based. So I didn't need to go out there and get 20 million people in my database—client base, not database. I needed to service every single person in my client base, really service them.

So if the rule is one in six are looking to buy or sell, and one in six know someone who's looking to buy or sell, you could double or triple that when it comes to investment and commercial. So if you're really communicating with your community and you're able to service them on any level— keep in mind that servicing may not be that you actually do the deal. There was a point where I didn't know what I was doing with industrial, or I didn't know what I was doing with a 1031, but having the network to be able to refer them to the right people, and after you refer and observe enough times, you learn how to do it. But being able to dig deep is something that I wish somebody had told me immediately. And then also build a team. Everybody wants to be a broker. I think the average profit on a team is about 40 percent. And the average profit for a broker is probably 25 percent or less.

Q: Oh, wow.

JM: Yeah. So there's not this glory like everyone thinks in being a broker. Growing a team is where you can just focus on what matters and being affiliated with a brokerage that provides a lot of that foundation, technology, and all of that. That is why I joined EXP.

Q: What inspires you?

JM: What inspires me at this point in life is self-actualization. When you start to realize all these limiting beliefs that you've had. I'll give you an example. I have been anywhere from 20- 40 pounds overweight through most of my adult life and sort of just blamed it on genetics. And then when I came into a "what I deserve" way of thinking, like, I deserve to be whatever image it is that works for you, because I don't subscribe to society's version of being overweight. But in my life, in my mind, and for who I want to be, I was 40 pounds overweight. Once I realized I deserve to be the image of what I want to be, I removed that limiting belief, I had a different mindset and then, boom, I lost 40 pounds.

And then being able to stay there and in hindsight, saying, "Wow, that was a limiting belief which I convinced myself of and knowing I deserved to be the version of me that I dream of, poof 40 lbs gone."

And the other thing that inspires me is just understanding that the whole world will conspire to keep you stuck where you are. They will say, "Oh, my God, Jenn, you do so much. You work hard, you're strong, you're healthy." Not in a negative, evil way or anything, but when you're a doer, people will automatically just be like, "You're doing enough. You can't quite possibly take that on or take this on or take that on." So it's self-actualization, which sounds selfish. And just knowing that it's actually okay to be selfish, which is easier when you have two daughters and a granddaughter. To model for them, the best version of you, is the best thing you can do for them.

I actually have a new granddaughter on my husband's side and two grandsons, but you know, being a role model, not even by choice, you just naturally are as a grandmother, it's okay to be completely selfish and to take care of yourself first. And it's okay to have self-actualization as what inspires you. Because if my granddaughter can get to that place now and not have to wait until she's 51, could you imagine what her life could be? NO LIMITS.

I have so many days of peace and joy, even though I challenge myself like nobody I know around me. Which is why I love being involved with this other group of women because, whoa, it's awesome to see how they challenge themselves.

At the age of 50, I finally gave up my crutches: alcohol, don't need it; binge watching, don't need it, well maybe once in a while. And it's not like I'm on some crazy kick. I'm just so into the work that I'm doing, into the positive things that I put in my own life. And that all comes from self-actualization, which I really do owe to one of my coaches Jon Cheplak. He just tends to live by example and, and you can't help if you really get involved with the coaching with him, come to that place, and then you're no longer able to live in that denial. So that's what inspires me—not by judgment or shame, but by living by example.

And even today for this interview, I'm not perfect because I'm in transition and wearing so many hats. I showed up, like, I have to be on video? My hair's a mess. This outfit is a mess. That's okay ,right? YES It is okay. And maybe fast forward two years from now, I'll have my makeup artist and my helicopter will fly me in for interviews, but hey it is all part of the journey.

Q: I love that you're so authentic. And I love how your story started and how it's progressed and you're not scared to learn and grow and do it imperfectly. It's perfectly imperfect. I love the way you explain that. I know you have a lot of things that are coming up. You're working on possibly moving to the Dominican Republic and all these kind of things. Are you still looking to grow a team?
JM: No, I'm not. I am not necessarily looking to grow a team. I will always be here in Real Estate for my friends, my family, and my existing and past clients. My daughter is licensed, so she'll probably take over a lot of that book of business. I will look to grow EXp and grow my coaching business alongside that. But not in direct sales. I've done a good 26 years, and not always perfectly, and then being in leadership and then running a brokerage. I've been at everybody's beck and call for so long. And it's too late to go back and build a team, that's just not where I'm at.

I want to continue to be present for my family, my friends. and I owe it all through this industry. In addition to my book of real estate business I want to be able to guide people, help people get unstuck and on the right track. I can help them to see their strengths and build a book of business beyond their wildest dreams. I'm super excited to be able to do that.

Q: And build a lifestyle that you really dream of. That's very important. I mean, hello, you work so hard and you never get there?

JM: Oh, my gosh, yes. I was single for 17 years and now I'm married for a year and a half. And my husband had a stroke the week before our wedding and then a whole series of other complications after the wedding. And then COVID hit him after he had lost 28 pounds. So I basically spent the best year of my life, professionally and personally, nursing my husband. And that's where Jon Cheplak's coaching really helped me so much. He didn't allow me to sit around and feel sorry for myself, because the whole world would've justified it, like, "Oh, my God, all these years, you finally found your partner and then…" Right? You could do that. And I didn't. With that help and with that guidance, none of my circumstances became an excuse. And both my daughters were in crisis and really needed me through the pandemic and after the pandemic, new mom and all that. I also was leading my local business community through the crisis and of course, the company I was COO for.

Q: It helped you get clear on what you really wanted.

JM: Exactly. Thank you. The lifestyle. I want to build and grow personally, professionally, financially within the parameters of the thing that first and foremost is my family and having a relationship with my husband and family that matters and that's loving and respecting and supportive and all of those things.

Q: This has been an amazing conversation. How can people find out more about Grit Assist or reach out to you for support or coaching?

JM: The website is www.Grit-Assist.com. On Instagram it's @GritAssistcoach or Jennmahermaher, Grit Assist or Jennifer Maher on Facebook. I'm easy to find. My email is Jenn@jennifermaher.com. I'll even give my cell phone number: (914) 330 7222. I love solving problems. I help people all the time without signing them up into coaching- to a degree. At some point you have to commit and have skin in the game. That's the one thing, it is really the financial commitment that helps you grow. You have no choice. Like I just doubled down. I took on new personal and business coaches, Bill Pipes and Janne Robinson, to make sure that I can build out this coaching business the way that I need to. And so although Grit-Assist is very reasonable, it's still an investment, which is important for people to make. But I look forward to helping lots of people.

Q: Jennifer, this has been amazing. Thank you so much for your time. And I cannot wait for everything we'll be doing together.

JM: Yes, me too.

JENNIFER MAHER
www.grit-assist.com

Jennifer Maher is a real estate powerhouse. She's been hooked on the industry since 1996, and has held many roles in the business. Jennifer approaches coaching and consulting from her unique perspective, gained from being an agent, broker, COO, property manager, team leader, landlord and investor.

Her extensive industry knowledge and passion for growth set her apart from other leaders in the field. Named one of Hudson Valley Magazine's Top Ten Women in Business in 2015, she was also awarded The Hudson Gateway Association of Realtors' Extra Mile Award in 2014.

Jennifer has always been a supporter and advocate for the business community and economic development in her region. She has served on the Executive board of both the Hudson Gateway and the Putnam County Association of Realtors, and is also the Immediate past & founding President of her local chapter of the New York State Commercial Association of Realtors. As founding past Chairwoman of the Putnam County Business Council, she served the business community as a persuasive advocate and liaison to Federal, State, and Local officials.

Jennifer has a long resume of helping Agents, Teamleaders and Brokers take their career and life to the next level. With expertise in team building, lead generation,community building, follow up and prospecting, Jennifer can help scale any business or project to the highest level possible. She is truly excited about helping others succeed,reach their goals and to do what she does best, get shit done.

It's okay to be completely selfish and to take care of yourself first. And it's okay to have self actualization.

—*Jennifer Maher*

MEGAN FARRELL-NELSON
The Megan Farrell Team
Real Estate Advisor/ Mentor

CHAPTER 16

Don't Quit Before The Magic Happens

with Megan Farrell-Nelson

HEY THERE, SUPERWOMEN. I AM SO EXCITED TODAY to talk to my next guest. She is an amazing real estate agent from Palm Coast, Florida. And you guys know that I have been talking to a lot of women in real estate and that I absolutely love real estate. So I really am excited to find out a little bit more about how our guest got into real estate, how she built her team, all the things. So let's get to it.

Q: Megan Farrell, how are you?
Megan Farrell-Nelson: Good. I'm good. Thanks so much for having me, Tam.

Q: How long have you been in real estate?
MN: I got in when I was 26. That's really young, relatively, for this career. I've been doing it for almost 10 years.

Q: I saw "26" and I thought, shoot, she looks 26 now. What made you decide that real estate was the career for you?
MN: Well, it's kind of funny that you ask that. Before I was in real estate, I was a kindergarten teacher. I was teaching a little bit farther north, and then life brought me to Florida. I took a break from teaching when I moved here. I knew I needed to take a break just to kind of re-land, and figure things out. You know, the mid-twenties, kind of "figuring-out-life phase." And not working sounds fun until you realize that everyone else works. It gets pretty boring when you're the only one not working.

Q: So true. That is hilarious.
MN: Also, as a person, I'm a doer, I'm a mover. I'm not sedentary. So eventually one of my friends who noticed I was bored and unhappy said to me, "Why don't you try real estate? You love people, you like talking." (Because those are the only skills you need, right? (Laughing)) So I decided to give it a shot! During my first year, I just fell in love with the business. I loved helping people solve their problems (needing to find a home/sell a home), getting creative in negotiations & helping people achieve their goals. That's really when I transitioned from being a kindergarten teacher and taking care of people's most valuable

possession, their baby, into helping people with their most valuable asset or investment, one of the most important things that they're going to purchase in their life, which is their home or their business.

So it was a natural transition. I fell in love with all that comes along with buying a home, just the emotional process, and connecting with people. My favorite part was having the conversation about where they're going to raise their little ones. It's also about setting yourself up financially. I'm a true believer that real estate is the foundation of wealth. Watching people grow their wealth with investment properties or even their primary residence is so rewarded. The business became really fun, really fast.

The age I was at was the perfect time for me to get into it. You know, in Florida, a lot of people come here to retire, obviously, and sometimes they end up doing real estate part-time or as a side gig. I was young! I was excited! I was energetic! (And still am) I jumped in with both feet. I didn't have a plan B so failure was not an option for me. I joke that if I knew how hard it was going to be then, I don't know if I would've started. Once I jumped and got in there, I kept moving forward. There's so much learning. Every single day brings new opportunities and new challenges, and I think that's the other part that's really exciting to me.

Q: That's really cool. Real estate is not easy. And you have to love it. Was your family or anyone that you know in real estate or even owned their own business?
MN: Yes. My father is actually a builder. So I grew up "in the industry" my whole life. My dad built homes. He ended up growing his business to do more commercial and medical buildings, but I grew up in houses and on Bobcats

and things like that. So, yeah, I guess helping people create "home" has always been a part of who I am.

Q: You've been in for almost 10 years and there have been a lot of ups and downs in business. Real estate is a very cyclical thing. What are some of the difficulties you have experienced as you grew and learned in your business?
MN: Well, I definitely had to get thick skin. That was really challenging for me. Like I said, I came from the kindergarten world where I taught children to be kind and to always do the right thing. The real estate industry can be pretty competitive and cutthroat at times. That was one of my biggest challenges, especially when I first got started, recognizing that everyone's not your friend and being okay with that.

Q: That's correct.
MN: That's a good life lesson that I got to take with me.

On the other side of the coin, the right people are for you! That's the real work I am doing now. I am learning to be my authentic self and that the right people are and will continue to walk with me. I learn a lot of life lessons through real estate. :)

And learning that it's not all about me! You know, in your twenties, you're self-involved. And so I had to learn that none of it is about me and I cannot control decisions being made by the buyers or the sellers. That made it easier to detach from the emotions of the transaction. People's moods? Not about me. What are the decisions made in regards to purchasing/selling? Not about me. It's not like my customers are buying or selling a pair of shoes, so I can't really *sell* anyone the house, right? I'm just facilitating the transaction based on what the customer is telling me and negotiating on their behalf. That was a pretty big lesson that was impactful at the beginning of my career, not just for business, but again, for life.

One of the biggest challenges that we have now is just controlling a narrative that is being put out there. Any day on any news source or any social media platform you can hear all sorts of fear mongering going on. "Rates are skyrocketing." "It's going to crash like in 2008." Being able to communicate effectively with my customers about facts and not feelings has been impactful for not just our business, but the general well-being and sometimes sanity of our customers (and selves). Improving my communication skills and listening has definitely been something I have focused on over the last 10 years. It allows me to be a better negotiator, to explain exactly what's going on throughout the transaction, and to help get the facts through to my customers when the outside noise gets loud.

Q: Yeah. We were talking right before we got started here, and one of the things that I love about what I do is that no matter what woman I speak to, whatever background she has, we have so many similarities. So I know that you've had to come through some difficulties in your own personal life and your health. Can you talk a little about that?
MN: Of course. When I got started in the industry, I was young, female, and single. I had to work very hard to prove myself, which led to me constantly trying to prove my value. I was overworked for the first 6 years of my career.

When I met my husband, he was actually a buyer. I like to joke that he bought the house and then I moved in. As my business and our relationship grew, the next logical step was to work together so he joined my real estate team in 2017, the year after we got married. When we had our son in 2019, I experienced severe postpartum depression. I would say that was probably the first really big personal challenge that I went through while in the industry.

At the time, I was the president of our local REALTOR association. I was chair for Florida REALTORS Young Professionals Network. Florida REALTORS is the largest trade organization in our state so I had some pretty big professional responsibilities on my plate. I also served on an additional 10+ professional & charitable committees and boards. I was trying to be all things to all people. The outside noise that I heard was people asking me if and when I was going to step down from these responsibilities since I had had our son. I fought so hard to prove that I wasn't going to "fail" or quit, that I COULD do it. In that process, I ended up losing Megan. I completely lost who I was- I had no hobbies, no deep personal relationships- I had stopped taking care of my health. Everything became about working and proving myself to anyone who was around.

Thankfully, I have an incredible husband that was so supportive, but there was only so much support he could provide his "independent" wife.

During that time, I was also in a business partnership with some people who I thought were smart, kind and good. I would soon find out that wasn't the case.

Due to my desire to achieve external success, I surrounded myself with people who I thought would take me to that next level. I ignored red flags, especially toward the end of the relationship because of the promises they were making to me and for our business. I was invited to attend a mastermind training event with those same business partners I trusted. I went there to learn and grow my business; there was more in store for me.

I ended up being drugged and sexually assaulted that weekend. It was the beginning of the most challenging two years of my life. These were people that I trusted. I had developed deep relationships with, both inside and outside of the industry. I thought my world was going to crumble.

It's something that I now call the best/worst weekend of my life, but seeing it that way took a long time. I sought out a relationship with my higher power and spoke with professionals. We all go through hard times. Everyone has stuff, right? This just happened to be mine. I played the victim for a long time. I wanted people to know how much I hurt and I wanted someone else to hurt like I did. So for about six months, I was not the best Megan that I possibly could be.

But then I did take time for myself. I went— I'm glad to share this part—I went to a treatment center for trauma. It's something I'm really proud of and I'm so grateful that I had the opportunity to do it. I was broken and so very hurt. If I didn't take that time for me, I would never have the life I have today, one that is beyond my wildest dreams. I couldn't even imagine being where we are today two years ago, or even three years ago. And through that experience, I also removed alcohol from my life. This wasn't something that had destroyed my life—yet. Who knows what path I could have continued on? Prior to this event, I had just started to look at the relationship I had with it and what it was doing (or not doing) for my life. Alcohol wasn't bringing me forward. It wasn't guiding me to be the woman I wanted to be. It wasn't allowing me to be the best mother, the best wife, the best friend. And so I removed that from my life and now it's been over 2 years. So that's super exciting.

Q: Megan, I just have to tell you, I am so grateful to have met you and that you felt comfortable enough to share that story, because there's so many women that have gone through trauma in their life, and I love the way you explained it. You took ownership of your own life, you went and got help and sought a way for you to not keep punishing yourself but instead to heal yourself and take responsibility for every part of your life. I've gone through things like that before, things that I was holding on to and didn't even realize that they were dictating a lot of the decisions I was making and I finally had to take ownership of it. So I really am so thankful that you shared that.

MN: Yeah. And I'm sorry that you went through that, but, you know, it's a funny paradox. I remember at first, someone telling me one day you're going to be grateful. And I'm like, that is the biggest crock of you know what. I thought there is absolutely no way that I could ever be grateful for this. Another thing that I was told was to pray for the people that hurt me. I honestly refused at the beginning. I had to start by praying for the willingness and soon everything began to change.

Now I would say at least once a week I'm praying for somebody that had a negative effect on my life. It's not for me to judge them, right? It's not for me to hold onto that.

I needed to get better for Megan. I need to get better for my three-year-old little boy. I need to be the best wife I can be. None of us asked for this, but they especially didn't.

We all have a thing, a vice in our life, that we know we need to quit. Whether it's drinking, drugs, exercising, eating, whatever it is! Something that if we gave it up our life would dramatically improve. Well, sometimes you can't stop for you. Sometimes you have to look around you and realize these people that you love love you so much and borrow the belief that you're worth making a change from them.

If I can't love myself right now through this, I'm going to borrow that belief from my boys and I'm going to borrow their love, and I'm going to love myself the best I can because they do. I lean on the people who are loving me while I'm going through it and I let myself rely on them. We all have a season that we need the people around us to be those rocks in the storm. Let your friends be your rocks because there will be a time when you need to be the rock for them. And those are the relationships that end up being the most impactful in our lives.

It's been a really beautiful journey. I didn't know that I'd ever say that either. If you are currently going through it, just know that there are days that are hard, but those days get fewer and farther between when you do the work and let time do its job. You deserve to heal and you deserve a great life. You can borrow my belief for you if you can't find it inside of you today.

Q: Yes. I love that. Oh, my goodness. What is inspiring you right now, Megan? In life or business or just in general?
MN: Oh, man, that little boy of mine. It's so fun being a mom of a three-year-old and everything is the coolest. Today they were cutting the grass in our backyard on a huge lawn mower. And he ran over to the door with both hands up on the window, eyes wide, like, wow, this is so cool. And he said, "Call Daddy! I want to tell Daddy!" And I was like, "All right, it's just a thing." And then the next thing is, like, "Oh, look at the dragonfly!" And then we're out there looking at ants and spiders and counting legs and all that stuff.

And I think him just being around that curious, energetic

little human has allowed me to also be a curious, energetic human. And he teaches me patience and to take a step back and recognize that when things go sideways it doesn't have to be a disaster. Like last night, my husband and I got a flat tire on our date night. Not convenient—but we called, got help, and were safe. And we were like, "All right, we're outside, there's no streetlights, let's look at these stars." And so it ended up being super romantic, right? When we first heard the tire, we were like, "Noooo." But that's life, right? The flat tires are life. It's all about taking that flat tire and making the best of the circumstances.

One thing that is non-negotiable if I want to have a great day is starting my morning with a sunrise walk or run along the ocean. I'm lucky enough to live by the beach and every morning the sunrise is different. The clouds are different, the lighting, the colors, all of it is different. And it reminds me that just as God had that time to paint a new sky in the morning, I have that opportunity to create whatever day I want. It's up to me how the rest of my day is going to go. Of course things happen that impact me and I'm disappointed and sad. I still have hard days. Taking that time for me in the morning starts my day off on the right foot. It allows me to be more patient with my real estate deals and to better manage other people's emotions. It just allows me to be a better human.

Q: I love it. What advice would you give to another woman who is trying to be successful in her life? Maybe she's starting out, maybe it's not going the way she wants, what advice would you give her?

MN: One of my favorite phrases: Don't quit before the magic happens.

Q: Oh, so good.

MN: It's a line that I heard many times in my recovery journey, and it's so powerful because it's so true. When I first got started in real estate, I did not have a supportive partner. And I can remember the days where I was working so hard, long hours, putting my head down and just trying and not seeing the reward. This happens at the beginning of everything. And so, I remember he was like, "When are you going to quit? When are you going to get a job?"

And I saw this little meme on social media and it was two men. And the man on top, he had his pickaxe, they were in dirt, and there was a whole thing of diamonds at the end. And the man had his pickaxe over his shoulder and his head down and he was walking back away from the diamonds; he had quit. And the other man was still going. And both of them were so close to the diamonds. But the first man quit and was walking away not knowing how close he was. And so I really try to carry that with me in every area of my life and business. I've been in real estate for years and years and our business has evolved. I was a single agent, now we have a team. We also opened a branch office for our company. We have over 15 agents who we are also mentoring and partially responsible for. So I try to remember, as I'm learning new skills, to grow those areas of my business as well, to remember that I'm always evolving and not to quit before that magic happens.

Q: Megan, this has been so good. Tell my listeners where they can find you on social media, where they can connect with you if they're in Florida, if they want to know more about real estate. What's the best way to contact you?

MN: All of my social media profiles are the same name: Megan Farrell-Nelson. And that is Facebook, Instagram,

LinkedIn. You can reach out to me on any of those platforms. I always reply to my messages. And that goes for any recovery stuff, too. Feel free to reach out if you have real estate questions, but if you're interested about reframing your relationship with alcohol or healing from past trauma, please also know you can contact me anytime.

Q: Thank you so much. It's been amazing talking to you. I cannot wait for all the stuff that we're doing.
MN: Yeah. Thank you, Tam.

MEGAN FARRELL-NELSON
www.themeganfarrellteam.com

Meet Megan; a 10 year veteran in the real estate industry! She escaped the snowy weather of Pennsylvania to live a life by the beach in Palm Coast, Florida. She and her husband, Brady, own & operate The Megan Farrell Team. Their primary goal is to provide a high level of customer service, while using their negotiation skills to help their customers achieve their real estate goals. This year they are on track to sell 100 homes & hit over $80,000,000 in career sales.

She runs a branch office for her company, REAL Broker, LLC, where she focuses on providing a positive environment where agents can thrive with collaboration over competition.

She is passionate about creating a positive real estate experience for all buyers and sellers. Her office tagline is #FindYourHappyPlaceFL, which is what she and Brady strive to help buyers & sellers and their agents do every day.

She recently celebrated 2 years alcohol free & is focused on becoming the best version of herself daily. If she's not doing any of the fun stuff mentioned above, you can find her on the beach with Brady & her 3 year old son, Elijah, drinking coffee & eating donuts.

Connect with Megan on all social platforms! @MeganFarrellNelson

Don't quit before
the magic happens.

—*Megan Farrell-Nelson*

SECTION 4

What's Next

TAM R. LUC
Delucslife Media, Women who BossUp,
Women with Vision International, CEO/ Founder

Real Estate is Sexy

with Tam Luc

I HAVE SAID THIS MORE THAN A HANDFUL OF times: Real estate is sexy.

I'm not sure when I first started saying it, but after a 22-year real estate career, I still say it. When I stopped being a flight attendant, I looked for a career where I could use my marketing skills and possibly continue to travel. I followed the advice of *Rich Dad Poor Dad* author Robert Kiyosaki and decided that real estate investing was where I wanted to be. Actually the dream was to open up Jamba Juice franchises in places like Hong Kong. Real estate seemed like a way to see the world and experience exciting new things.

Real estate is one of those careers that allows you to find your place no matter what your interest is. I started out in residential real estate and moved into commercial, because I thought I could learn so much more there. I also got my residential real estate license in the state of California in case I needed to sell homes. That never happened. Most of my career was spent in operations and marketing.

One thing was always clear to me: Real estate is a very good career for women. Women have many needs that are different from men and real estate gives us the flexibility to raise our families. Even without a formal education, real estate gives you the opportunity to be extremely successful if you're willing to work. It is not an easy career but it certainly is an amazing career that you can experience in many different ways.

So how did this book come about? When I started thinking about creating this collection of interviews, I was so excited because of my background in real estate. If there was one sure way that I could show an example of Women Who BossUp, I knew it would be in real estate. Some of the most successful women in the world are in real estate. Actually real estate is a great career for men or women, but I knew that with real estate I could really show a woman what it looks like to dream big and create the lifestyle that she wants.

There are so many auxiliary careers to explore within the field as well. When you read through this book, you will get an idea of how much is possible. I hope you walk away with this: "If they can do it, so can I." Read through the stories of trials and struggles. Connect with the similarities between your life and theirs. Realize that you can dream about what you want and you can make it happen. They did it, and so can you.

Keep pushing and remember to keep bossing up.

TAM LUC

www.delucslife.com

After years of struggling in business and experiencing the ups and downs of life. Tam speaks on what finally turned her life around and how she created a multi-six figure business in less than 2 years. She shares her secrets on how anyone can use their own story to nail their core message and create a huge impact in the world.

Number one bestselling author of *A Women's Side Hustle* and the *Women Who BossUp* book series, International Speaker with 22 years of entrepreneurial and investment experience now giving her heart to doing what she loves for women that are working hard to find their way.

Follow Up Boss

IS A PROUD SUPPORTER OF

WOMEN WHO BOSS UP IN REAL ESTATE

BOSS UP BY USING **FOLLOW UP BOSS** TO STREAMLINE YOUR LEADS & TO TAKE CONTROL OF YOUR FOLLOW UP. WORK SMARTER, DELIVER A FIRST-CLASS CLIENT EXPERIENCE & CLOSE MORE DEALS!

---

followupboss.com

Are You Tired Of Being The World's Best Kept Secret?...
Then You'll Love..

The Women Who BossUp

Talk of the Town

Visibility is The Key To Growing Your Business!

ARE YOU READY TO BOSS UP?

This isn't like any PR or Media package you have ever seen....

LIMITED SPOTS AVAILABLE!

If you desire to...

✓ Create credibility and influence to ELEVATE YOUR BRAND

✓ Get QUALIFIED EXPOSURE for your business and consistent traffic to your website.

✓ Build a COMMUNITY OF SUPER FANS that will want to hire you, buy from you and refer business to you.

THEN, THIS IS FOR YOU!

TO LEARN MORE VISIT

www.bossupbestseller.com/talkofthetown

HIRE A VIRTUAL ASSISTANT TODAY!

BOOK YOUR FREE CONSULTATION

www.sphererocketva.com

OUR SERVICES

ACCELERATOR PROGRAM

- Unlimited VA's
- Advanced Coaching & Training
- Private Mastermind
- FREE Membership through Referrals

Accelerator Program is a program that's designed for businesses to scale by using more virtual assistants.

SPHEREROCKET
ACCELERATOR

f sphererocketva ⊙ sphererocketva ▶ Sphere Rocket Real Estate Virtual Assistants

SunQuest Funding

Uneasy about the mortgage process? We can help!

We put YOU first!

We offer the Four C Mortgage Process Committment:

1. **Clarity:** We keep things transparent, remove any mystery from the process and walk you through it.

2. **Communication:** We'll keep you informed every step of the way.

3. **Confidence:** We use the most secure, high-tech application platform available, so you can be sure your data is safe.

4. **Competence:** Our highly experienced staff will get you an answer fast, and you'll work with the same person throughout the entire process.

For more information, scan the QR Code above or call 908-272-8330.

Elevate Your
Expectations

At Stewart, helping you deliver smooth customer experiences is our main priority. We listen closely, respond quickly and address the unique circumstances of every transaction to ensure your closings are the celebratory experience you and your clients deserve. You can count on us to provide the latest industry insights, technology, tools and training to help grow your business. We're the partner committed to giving you more.

Work with the title company that gives you more.

Stewart Title Company
Anthony R. Coppola, Jr.
NJ State Sales Manager
973.334.2735 office
732.558.5855 mobile

stewart.com

///▲Stewart
TITLE

LET'S BE
Social

@womenwithvisioninternational

Do you have a BossUp moment in your life?
We want to hear your story.

Email us at: support@delucslife.com